jad

PUBLISHING

Genocide in Sudan:

Caliphate threatens Africa and the world

Genocide in Sudan:

Caliphate threatens Africa and the world

Lt. General Abakar M. Abdallah

Jerome B. Gordon

Deborah P. Martin

Published by JAD Publishing, LLC

615 Bayshore Drive

Pensacola, Florida 32507

Cover Art and Design by Kendra Mallock

ISBN: 978-0-692-94539-1

First Edition

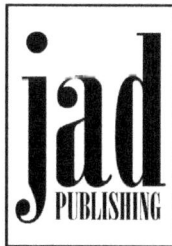

www.jadpublishing.com

Dedication

We dedicate this volume to the people who have died in this ongoing genocide in Sudan since 1881 when Mohammed Mahdi, the self proclaimed Islamic Messiah, declared Sharia law, issued a Jihad fatwa in Sudan and began a campaign to cleanse the country from infidels, as he believed should be done. This phenomenon is continuing today as children hide in caves and run from rampaging Arab militias, whether mounted on horses, camels or heavily armed pick-up trucks, in the hope they will not be shot, captured, slaughtered, thrown into a burning fire or raped.

We honor all marginalized people of Sudan who are continually suffering under the brutal successive dictatorship of International Criminal Court-indicted Sudan President Omar Ahmad Hassan al-Bashir and the Muslim Brotherhood (National Islamic Front / National Congress Party) regimes that have ruled Sudan since 1989.

We honor all Sudanese who suffer under this regime especially, people of Darfur, Nuba Mountains, Beja, Nubia, Blue Nile and Abyei. Further, we honor the South Sudanese who are still bearing the suffering of Sudan's regime. The peoples of Sudan and South Sudan collectively are resisting the annihilation of their peoples under the genocidal policies of The Republic of the Sudan. They bear the daily threat of annihilation by the Bashir government, which must be stopped for the genocide to end.

Finally, we honor those American stalwart supporters of the human rights of indigenous African peoples of Sudan: Eric Reeves, Ryan Boyette and Dr. Tony Catena and former US Virginia Congressman Frank Wolf and founding co-chair of Congressional Human Rights Caucus.

CONTENTS

Preface and Acknowledgements

"Far from being moribund, Mohammedanism is a militant and proselytizing faith. It has already spread throughout Central Africa, raising fearless warriors at every step; and were it not that Christianity is sheltered in the strong arms of science—the science against which it had vainly struggled—the civilization of modern Europe might fall, as fell the civilization of ancient Rome."

- Winston S. Churchill, The River War

Those observations by the young intrepid journalist and former British Subaltern Winston Churchill from his chronicle of the Anglo-Egyptian war against Mohammed Mahdi in the Sudan ring true in the 21st Century. For the descendants of the Arab tribes in Sudan are being gathered by International Criminal Court-indicted war criminal President Omar al-Bashir to form a veritable army of Mujahideen from across the Sahel region of Africa and veterans of the Islamic State to achieve the objective of the Mahdi, leader of a Sharia supremacist caliphate ruled from Khartoum. A Caliphate backed by billions of dollars of funding from Saudi Arabia, the Gulf Coast Cooperation Emirates seeking to create a breadbasket for the Middle East in the Sudan and earn billions from development and exploitation of the country's mineral and energy wealth.

This is furthered by Sudan's active participation, with backing from its Muslim Brotherhood partner, the wealthy Persian Gulf emirate of Qatar that provides weapons and billions in funding to train and equip a 150,000-man Arab Rapid Support Force Janjaweed mercenary army. The Sudan Qatar partnership has been actively engaged supporting the overthrow of adjacent regimes in Libya, Chad and the Central African Republic.

That jihadist Army, under the direct control of the regime's National Intelligence and Security Service, has been deployed in the conflict zones of Darfur, Nuba Mountains and Blue Nile State with the objective of completing the genocidal ethnic cleansing of indigenous black African people to exploit the region's agricultural and natural resources wealth.

As we write the estimate of those killed may have exceeded more than 600,000 and approximately 5 million have been displaced internally with virtually no protection against the rampages of the RSF/Janjaweed burning villages, raping women, killing men, seizing animals, destroying crops. Moreover, those in internal displaced persons camps have no protection from the UNAMID. Several hundred thousand have fled the country to UN Refugee Camps in neighboring Chad and the Central African Republic. Realize that there not been a formal census of Sudan since late 1980's. Further, the Bashir regime does not count the number of dead indigenous Sudanese.

The 2020 target date for completion of this agenda was laid out in the so-called Arab Coalition Plan captured by one of the co-authors from an RSF/Janjaweed vehicle in 2014 in Darfur.

This book documents the continuing war of annihilation against indigenous black African people in Sudan and the threat of spreading state sponsored jihadist overthrow of adjacent regimes in North and Central Africa. It is derived, in part, from a compilation of articles published in the *New English Review, FrontPage Magazine, Fitnaphobia* and other publications as well as original source information, such as the Arab Coalition Plan in Appendix B and the secret minutes of the Sudan National Political Crisis Committee in Appendix C.

The authors of this volume would like to acknowledge all the Sudanese and South Sudanese who have participated directly in sharing their lives and stories honestly in order to bring us to write this book. Without their cooperation, kindness, honor, forthrightness and courage, there would be no words to put on these pages.

Thank you all!

Chapter One
Could Sudan be the cornerstone of the Caliphate in Africa?

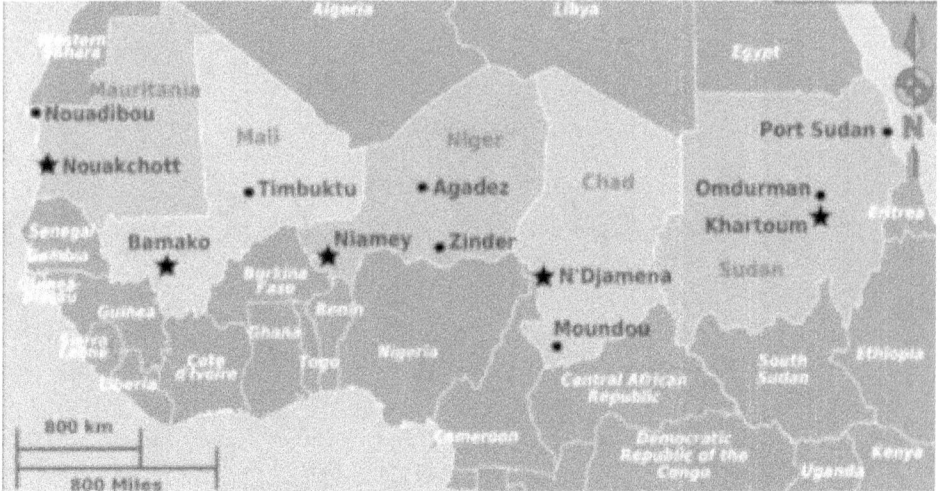

The Islamic Republic of the Sudan Objective is to Establish a Caliphate Composed of Sudan, Chad, Central African Republic, Niger and Mali

Just after the election of President-elect Donald Trump on November 8, 2016, Dr. Walid Phares, his principal advisor on Middle East Affairs, spoke before a group of American Sudanese Nuba émigrés in Washington, DC. Eric Reeves of Amnesty International wrote in a November 15, 2016 column in the *Sudan Times* about Phares' statement. He speculated on what the Trump Administration might accomplish in the first 100 days to address the genocide by the corrupt Bashir regime:

> He said America under the leadership of Donald Trump would not tolerate what he called abuses practiced by the Khartoum government against its own citizens. Furthermore, he added that there is no reason why the United States and its European allies should lift the economic sanctions on Bashir's regime established in 1997 in light of the continued violations in Sudan. Moreover, Mr. Walid Phares indicated that they will work with the

international community during the first hundred days to end the crisis in Darfur, Blue Nile and South Kordofan.

Mahmoud A. Suleiman wrote about the duplicity of President Bashir's outreach to President–elect Trump, in another *Sudan Times* op-ed, "Bashir's call for mutual cooperation with U.S. Trump:"

> It is pathetic that Omer al-Bashir offered congratulations to the U.S. President-elect Donald Trump and looked forward to cooperate with the new US president. The NCP Génocidaire Omer Hassan Ahmed al- Bashir forgot or ignored the mere promise of achieving democracy for the people of Sudan. This style of political discourse is not surprising in the era of the unratified [27-year] ruling regime of the National Congress Party (NCP). The regime has decided during the so-called Wathba dialogue or National Dialogue Conference in Khartoum on October 10, 2016 that Omer al-Bashir will continue as President of Sudan until the year 2020 without being democratically elected by the disenfranchised. There is no comparison between this and what happens in the United States of America. The comparison between what is followed democratically in the United States of America and the dictatorship in Sudan is neither fair nor appropriate.

President–elect Donald Trump confirmed during most of his campaign that he would declare the war on radical Islam. The peaceful way employed by President Barack Obama in his diplomatic relations with the radical Islamist duo, Khartoum and Tehran, and called the "Obama's approach", was exploited by the Sudanese regime and Iranian governments and seems to have approached the end. Since the Islamic countries found in the Obama regime simply a break from the George W. Bush Presidency's ultimatum that puts clear: "either with us or against us". Thus, that honeymoon period might be approaching an end.

President Bashir wrote President-elect Trump as the 'duly elected' President of the Islamic Republic Sudan. His faux election in 2011 was conducted in accordance to Sharia in that only Muslims in the Khartoum capital region could vote for him as President of the NCP regime. African tribes elsewhere in the Sudan (Darfur, South Kordofan regions) are not considered Muslims and therefore ineligible to vote. The NCP Khartoum central government propaganda is that these regions do not recognize the fraudulent election of President Bashir, which it contends, is recognized as the 'legitimate' government, internationally.

The problem that the incoming Trump Administration faces is that President Bashir is mobilizing an enormous Jihad army poised to perpetrate the final destruction of resistance forces in both the Darfur and South Kordofan regions of the Sudan has begun. Bashir and his National Congress Party (NCP) led government unleashed renewed attacks on November 24, 2016 in the Nuba region of South Kordofan, a prelude to conquering the area. At the same time, he was facing civil unrest in the capital of Khartoum, where troops had prepared mass graves for the expected slaughter of protesters over the failure of his domestic economic policies. Opposition in Khartoum had called for a three-day strike, reported on November 27, 2016, protesting fuel shortages. The Bashir security forces used tear gas against protesters with worse consequences to come.

His agenda is to cleanse these regions of African tribes for resettlement by the families of the Orwellian-named "Peace Force', formerly the Janjaweed, composed of foreign mercenaries, and to exploit precious metals resources in the Nuba Mountains and Jebel Amir gold mines in North Darfur. The Khartoum regime 'ethnic cleansing' of Darfurians in the Jebel Marra region was described in detail by Gen. Abdallah in our November 2016 *New English Review* interview with him, "Only Regime Change Can Stop Sudan's Genocide." What follows is a situation report (SITREP) on what is happening in Sudan. The corrupt Islamist regime of indicted war criminal President Omar al-Bashir seeks with Arab countries financing and support to create a massive Jihad army. He has launched a campaign to create by armed force a Caliphate across sub Saharan Africa ruled under Islamic Sharia law.

Mobilization of 150,000 men to complete Destruction of Darfur, Nuba and Establish Caliphate

The Sudan regime uses tribes and terrorist groups to fight proxy wars for the benefit of the National Congress Party (NCP) regime in Khartoum and Arab Coalition partners. In January 2016, the Khartoum government mobilized 9,000 men composed of Janjaweed militias, ISIS operatives, Lord Resistance Army (LRA) fighters from Uganda, Boko Haram of Nigeria, al Shabab of Somalia, Mali Jihadists, and Sudanese armed forces. The combined force attacked Jebel Marra using chemical weapons. Since then, the recruitment has not stopped as the regime continues to recruit people from Arab tribes and bring in foreign terrorists to fight beside the Sudanese government army. Over the 15-year-old Darfur crisis, the NCP regime mobilized each year Arab militia forces of 10,000 to 30,000. However, the mobilization this time is different in terms of numbers, parties involved, and overall objectives.

The regime has changed the name of the Rapid Support Forces into Kuat al Salam (Peace Forces). The new recruitment is being done under the name of the so-called Peace Forces. The reason for the name change was to eradicate the references the Janjaweed and Rapid Support Forces that most people in Darfur and the international community knew were committing genocide, war crimes, and human right abuses. The name change amounts to Orwellian Islamic *taqiyyah* –religiously condoned dissimilitude- lying for Allah - to deceive people in order to join up for training especially among non-Arab youths.

The regime's strategy is to mobilize 150,000 men for the Darfur attack to eradicate the people of Darfur and overthrow the adjacent government of Chad. They said that all Zaghawa are the same and even if they killed all Zaghawa of Darfur (Sudan) and left those of Chad they have done nothing. The objective behind this massive mobilization of a veritable Jihad army of 150,000 men is to destroy all Zaghawa and overthrow the governments of Chad, Niger, Mali, South Sudan, and the Central African Republic establishing a Caliphate in Sub Sahara Africa. There are an estimated 400,000 Zaghawa African Muslim pastoralist people spread over Darfur in Western Sudan (145,000), Chad (271,000) and Libya (10,000). The name Zaghawa is derived from the type of sheep raised by the ethnic group. They usually refer to themselves as the Beri people. The Tuareg Jihadist Ansar Dine group operating in Azawad region in Northern Mali is tasked to take over Mali. Some factions of the SELEKA rebels commanded by people of Arab origin will be tasked to liberate the Central Africa Republic. The plan is that South Sudan will be liberated by Riek Machar and supported by South Sudan Islamic Liberation Movement led by Ali Tamim Fartak. Fartak was a member of Muslim Brotherhood Organization and National Congress Party prior to South Sudan independence. There are also 8,000 militiamen currently grouped in D'ean, Eastern Darfur region prepared to attack South Sudan.

If that objective were attainable, it would change the map of Africa. The area from South Sudan to Mali would constitute an African Caliphate. The Khartoum regime is preparing to field this massive Jihad Army to fight and occupy this swath of sub-Saharan Africa to be administered under Sharia Islamic law.

Saudi Arabia, Kuwait, and Qatar would provide funding and political guidance, while Sudan would organize the Jihad mercenary army, conduct training, and provide operational control. Training camps are located in the Azawad region of Mali, Libya and Darfur.

According to our sources Sudan mobilized 30,000 men in Darfur and recruited thousands of others in both Sudan and contiguous Chad. Khartoum airdropped supplies of weapons such as AK-47s and RGPs for this basic force. They provided 2,500 Toyota Hi-lux pickup trucks that will be used for military operations, and 500 additional Toyota vehicles are on the way.

In order for the Khartoum regime to achieve its recruitment goal, they openly recruited men for the 'Peace Forces' in Darfur. They have also secretly recruited personnel in Chad and sent them to Sudan for training. They are exploiting the current financial crisis of the government of Chad. For months now people have not received their salaries and there is anger. People are protesting against the government. The Khartoum regime pays 30,000 SDG per person and a similar amount or more to middlemen.

In Chad the payment to recruits for the so-called Peace Force varies. It is based on the different status of an individual as between cadre and an ordinary recruit. For some cadres they pay a million CFA about $2,000 US while others receive 500,000 CFA, which amounts to about $1,000 US dollars. Cadres that cannot travel directly to Sudan are sent to West African States of Niger, Senegal etc. and from there fly to Sudan. The operation is well coordinated with Sudan, Saudi Arabia, Kuwait and Qatar governments, and is supported by political parties and private organizations in Chad.

There is one political party named Militants' Party for Unity and Development (Parti des Militants pour l'Unité et Development). Khalil Ali Osman is the leader of the political party and he is the overall coordinator of these different groups of militias and terrorists operating in Darfur, the Azawad Region of Mali, and Libya. There is another member of the same political party in charge of foreign relations. He coordinates activities with Saudi Arabia, Qatar, and Kuwait. There is also an organization called Defense and Development of Arabic Language in Chad working together with the above mentioned political party. They organize conferences and invite Arab governments and individuals from Gulf States to raise funds.

Our sources also said that they opened centers in different places in Darfur to teach French language to their militia forces, so that when they occupied Chad, Niger, and Mali they will not be having language problems.

About 5,000 Chadian rebels completed their training with Libyan Islamic groups, possibly Fajir Libya, which the Sudan government supports. They are waiting for deployment. They moved this Chadian rebel force from Sudan to Libya between late July and August of 2016.

As of this report militias changed the name of Kutum, North Darfur into Waha and declared it a liberated area of Janjaweed, now renamed "Peace Force."

As an example of the brutality of this "Peace Force," there is a man called Dr. Abdallah who lives in Geinena, Western Darfur, in charge of Hakamas (women who sing war songs to encourage fighters). Reportedly, he has told the Janjaweed militias that no Hakamas will sing for anyone who did not kill one hundred people. Each militiaman must bring body parts for hundred people to allow Hakamas to sing for him.

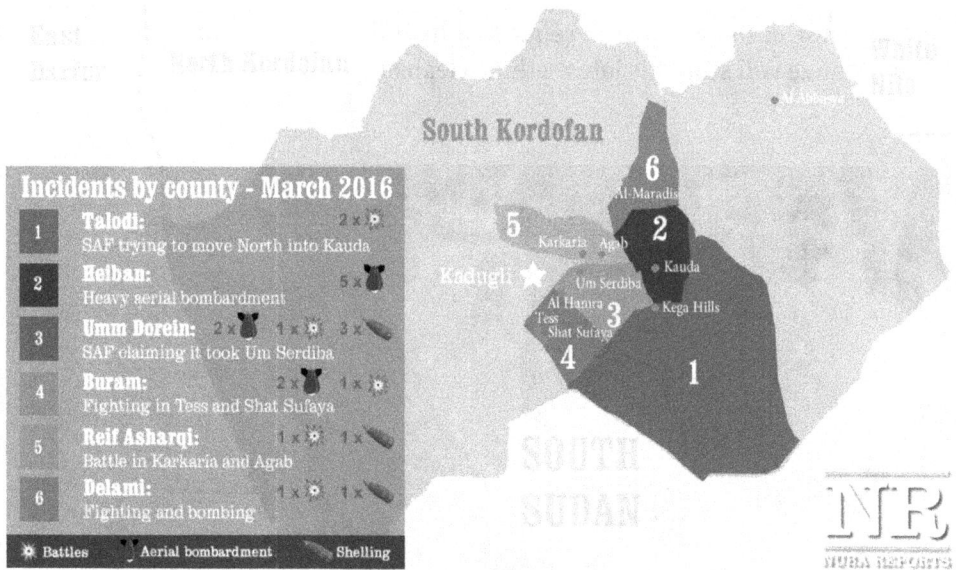

Incidents by county - March 2016

1. **Talodi:** 2 x [battle]
   SAF trying to move North into Kauda
2. **Helban:** 5 x [aerial bombardment]
   Heavy aerial bombardment
3. **Umm Dorein:** 2 x [aerial bombardment] 1 x [battle] 3 x [shelling]
   SAF claiming it took Um Serdiba
4. **Buram:** 2 x [aerial bombardment] 1 x [battle]
   Fighting in Tess and Shat Sufaya
5. **Reif Asharqi:** 1 x [battle] 1 x [shelling]
   Battle in Karkaria and Agab
6. **Delami:** 1 x [battle] 1 x [shelling]
   Fighting and bombing

[battle] Battles [aerial bombardment] Aerial bombardment [shelling] Shelling

Nuba Mountain battle map. Unleashing the attack on the Nuba Region

The Sudanese Government and militias have massed forces for an invasion of the Nuba Mountains in South Kordofan. There are upwards of 8 training camps in the area of Kordofan that have trained 15,000 international jihadists, about 2,000 trainees per camp. These mujahedeen are part of the invading force in Nuba. The majority of these mujahedeen are from Syria. Additional mujahedeen recruits are flooding into Sudan from the Middle East to join the proposed Caliphate to fight against the West. They believe they must cleanse the land of Abiid (black, indigenous, African) people. Abiid in Arabic means, "slave." When these jihadists have graduated training they will join the battle in the Nuba Mountains in order to accomplish ethnic cleansing of the land. After training these Mujahideen, they joined the heavily armed Sudanese government force in Kordofan in December 2016 and January 2017 when the full Kordofan cleansing operation   began.

Reports from Kadugli, Sudan, capitol city of Nuba Mountains, indicate that the heavily armed militia now outnumbers the remaining citizens, approximately 500 people.   Kadugli once hosted 300,000 inhabitants prior to the 2012 massacre by Sudan Armed Forces bombing raids. The current estimated population is approximately 94,000. The militia is there to build a factory to produce enough cyanide for Khartoum's gold production needs from deposits in the Nuba Mountains. The current push that began on November 24, 2016 is directed at ethnically cleansing the Umm Derien area. See area 3 on the Nuba battle map. The remaining people have protested and been threatened by the militia with death. The Khartoum regime will likely order the militia push to 'neutralize'   the   protesters.

The Governor of the Nuba area requested help from the outside world but only regime change will stop this latest ethnic cleansing massacre in 2016.

Sudan's President Omar Al-Bashir visits Saudi King Salman Riyadh November 2015

The Saudi Sudan Connections – Money for Switching Sides

One of the strategic aspects of this latest wave of ethnic cleansing in both the Darfur in Western Sudan and in the Nuba Mountains in South Kordofan is motivated by the exploitation of gold deposits. Further, we noted the backing of Saudi Arabia and Emeriti members of the Gulf Cooperation Council behind possible creation of a Caliphate in the Sahel region of Sub-Saharan Africa.

There are several developments arising from the sudden switch of Sudan, as the only Sunni country in the horn of Africa, to have been a long-standing ally of the Shi'ite Islamic Republic of Iran. Iran had assisted the Sudan in creating a munitions industry. Sudan had facilitated transshipment of Iranian weapons to other Sunni proxies, Hamas and Palestinian Islamic Jihad in Gaza. That prompted periodic Israeli air attacks on convoys transiting from Port Sudan across Egypt's Sinai Peninsula, as well as interdiction of Iranian arms cargoes in the Red Sea. Moreover, Sudan had been a major state supporter of terrorism providing training camps for Osama bin Laden. It had also previously supplied weapons for the Shia Houthi insurgency in Yemen across the Bab al Mandab straits in the Red Sea.

Sudan faced onerous fiscal isolation caused by nearly 20 years of international sanctions, the loss of substantial oil revenues with the founding of the independent Republic of South Sudan and civil war there. Khartoum found itself in dire financial straits facing internal unrest and protests over its faltering economic policies. Military and security expenditures claimed fully 70 percent of Sudan's dwindling budget. What to do?

19

The answer was to switch sides and opt for major Saudi financial support and investment in precious metals development both offshore in the Red Sea and on-shore in both North Darfur and the Nuba Mountains. That switch took place in 2014 when Sudan closed Iranian and Shia cultural centers in Khartoum. In 2015, with the Bashir regime sent 6,000 troops with supporting aircraft to provide boots on the ground in the Saudi and GCC air campaign against the Iranian backed Houthi rebels. The Iran-supported Shiite Houthi had ousted the Yemeni government of Saudi ally, President Abdrabbuh Mansur Hadi. The Saudi Kingdom provided a $5 billion military aid package to Khartoum. Riyadh invested in the Atlantis II Red Sea bed mineral extraction project. It may produce a $20 billion profit for the Saudi Kingdom under its so-called modernization program aimed at reducing reliance on oil revenues. Riyadh further bolstered its financial support to both Djibouti and Somalia in the Horn of Africa.

Eleonora Ardemagni an international relations analyst of the Middle East, focused on Yemen and the GCC region, noted these developments in an April 2016 article published by The Arab Gulf States Institute in Washington, DC, "The Yemeni Factor in the Saudi Arabia Sudan Realignment". She summarized the financial benefits to Khartoum from switching sides:

> The Saudi-Sudanese realignment is based on a "money for proxies" informal pact: external financial-military aid from Riyadh to Khartoum in exchange for direct military commitment of Sudanese troops for overseas operations. Such military interdependence has also boosted economic ties and joint projects between Sudan and Saudi Arabia, as well as other Arab Gulf states. This includes Sudanese gold production and the exploitation of offshore mineral resources in the Red Sea, where Saudi Arabia and Sudan share a common area, the Atlantis II joint venture. In 2015, the Sudanese central bank received $1 billion from Saudi Arabia and, previously, $1.22 billion dollars from Qatar. Riyadh and Abu Dhabi hosted the Saudi-Sudanese and the UAE-Sudanese Investment Forum, respectively. On November 2015, Saudi Arabia committed $1.7 billion for the building of three dams in northern Sudan, to be constructed within five years, plus $500 million for water and electricity projects and the cultivation of agricultural land in eastern Sudan.

With the influx of billions in Saudi and GCC funds, Khartoum now has the financial underwriting for its 'final solution' for Darfur and South Kordofan giving it a free hand to exploit their gold deposits. Perhaps the long sought gold production in these regions might back its faltering currency. Moreover, the profits from joint ventures with the Saudis would aid in launching its mercenary Jihad Army to create a Caliphate across most of the Sahel region of sub–Saharan

Africa. It also may have the Saudi Kingdom's support to intercede on its behalf to end the 20-year international sanctions regime. The Saudi and GCC backing may also effectively stifle the International Criminal Courts outstanding warrant for the arrest of Sudan's President for war crimes in Darfur. That has already happened with South Africa's refusal to arrest Bashir during a state visit and a recent announcement by the OAU that it is capable of trying dictatorial leaders of member countries for "crimes against humanity", as in the case of the former Chadian despotic leader.

Conclusion

President Bashir and his NCP government members were hoping that Hillary Clinton was going to win the US Presidential election. If Clinton won, they believed that she would continue Obama's policies that embraced the Khartoum regime. However, President-elect Donald Trump surprised them. So they are preparing to quickly finish their operation between now and first 100 days of the Trump Administration following his inauguration on January 21, 2017.

Sudan, Saudi Arabia, Kuwait, and Qatar are sources of financing terrorists that cause instability in Africa and the world. They are also the countries that currently cause instability in South Sudan, Mali, Niger, Chad, Nigeria, Cameroon, Libya, as well as the Sudan regions of Darfur, Kordofan, and Blue Nile. They pose a threat to international peace and security. Sudan's regime is playing the role of late Libyan Leader Gaddafi who destabilized Chad for more than thirty years in an attempt to expand Arab territory in Sub-Saharan Africa. We urge the international community, especially United States and countries that are fighting the global war on terrorism, to take seriously this SITREP and deal with the Islamist Sudan of indicted war criminal President Omar al-Bashir.

Chapter Two
Peacemaking Calumny

At the start of the fighting season in Sudan in November 2016, outgoing US Ambassador and Special Envoy to Sudan and South Sudan, Donald Booth, published a column on November 22, 2016 in the *Sudan Tribune*, which we present here, on the Darfur Crisis addressed to the Chairman of the Sudan Liberation Movement (SLM), Abdul Wahid al-Nour. Ambassador Booth chided Abdul Wahid for not joining other Darfuri armed resistance groups in refraining from resistance operations and joining peace negotiations with the Islamist Republic of Sudan regime in Khartoum of President Omar al-Bashir, who has ruled for 27 years following a military coup. Although at the same time, Ambassador Booth admits he can understand why Abdul Wahid is skeptical of any worthwhile outcomes for his leaving exile in Paris amid new developments of a massive effort by President Bashir and his NCP regime to launch massive 'ethnic cleansing' operations in Darfur and the Nuba Mountains.

We, also, obtained permission to publish the rebuttal, which appears below, of SLM Chairman Abdul Wahid to Ambassador Booth's *Sudan Tribune* column.

US Ambassador and Special Envoy to Sudan and South Sudan, Donald Booth

"Peace in Sudan must not be held hostage to Abdul Wahid," *Sudan Tribune*, November 22, 2016, by US Ambassador and Special Envoy to Sudan and South Sudan, Donald Booth.

Abdul Wahid al-Nour, leader of one of Sudan's armed opposition groups, has not set foot in his country in over a decade. He spends most of his time directing his armed group in Darfur from a satellite phone in his Paris apartment. His refusal to negotiate has been a perennial problem for international efforts to end the conflict in Sudan, but it has become especially damaging as other parties to the conflict begin moving toward peace.

On October 31, 2016, three of the four most prominent armed groups in Sudan committed to a unilateral, six-month cessation of hostilities following a similar commitment from the Sudanese government. While such declarations are not new to Sudan, it is unusual for parties to make that commitment at the outset of the fighting seasons (the dry season in Darfur). In recent months, we have also seen, with the notable exception of the area of Darfur under Abdul Wahid's control, a reduction in violence and bellicose rhetoric from the negotiating parties.

Yet, Abdul Wahid refuses to commit to even a temporary halt in fighting for humanitarian aid to reach the people of Jebel Marra, and he has refused overtures to negotiate with the Government of Sudan or participate in consultations to end the violence. He refused to take part in the Arusha Consultations of August 2007, the Sirte Conference of November 2007, the unification initiative in N'Djamena and Addis Ababa in July-August 2009, and the AU-UN/Qatar Initiative in Doha from 2009-2011.

Abdul Wahid has also boycotted all of the more recent initiatives to end Sudan's conflicts, including an African Union-led process and recent meetings in Kampala overseen by President Museveni. In August, the leaders of some of the largest armed and unarmed opposition groups signed the Africa Union-drafted 'roadmap' for future political negotiations, which was previously signed by the government. But Abdul Wahid did not attend.

To be fair, Abdul Wahid has valid reasons to be skeptical of the political process and to distrust a government that has bombed and displaced his people for over a decade. Recent arrests of opposition political party officials in Khartoum are a disturbing setback for those trying to engage in peaceful political competition. But Abdul Wahid's exclusively military strategy has not advanced his cause and has enabled continued violence to devastate his homeland. Abdul Wahid's refusal to grant UN peacekeepers permission to address claims of government attacks against civilians in areas that he controls is incomprehensible.

Peace in Sudan must not be held hostage to Abdul Wahid's refusal to engage. What is needed is an inclusive and comprehensive peace process that involves all actors and addresses the political, security, and humanitarian issues at the root of Sudan's conflicts. The people of Sudan, and above all the people of Jebel Mara, need Abdul Wahid at the table.

In my own recent visits to Darfur, I spoke with several groups of displaced Darfuris who all said the same thing. They just want the fighting to stop.

It is time for Abdul Wahid to join other opposition groups by declaring a unilateral cessation of hostilities, committing to political negotiations, and engaging in genuine efforts to end years of unspeakable violence.

Donald Booth was the former United States Special Envoy for Sudan and South Sudan

Events after Envoy Donald Booth's visit

During the tour of US Special Envoy Donald Booth to Darfur, anyone who spoke with him was arrested. Alrasheed Eissa, an employee of the UNAMID and Mayor of Nertiti, was arrested with many others on July 31, 2016 after a meeting with Envoy Booth on July 28, 2016. Eissa was released from jail on August 12, 2016, having been accused of being a member of the resistance.

Alrasheed Eissa, an employee of the UNAMID in Nertiti and the Mayor of Nertiti, Darfur

Mohamed Eltigani Saifeldeeni detainee. Free after 1 year 29 days in confinement

Mohamed Eltigani Saifeldeeni, had also been arrested by Khartoum forces on July 31, 2016 after the same meeting with Envoy Booth on July 28, 2016, was the most recently released detainee. He just celebrated his release on August 29, 2017 after 1 year 29 days in confinement!

More information on the Darfurian men still held in custody is contained in Appendix D.

Abdul Wahid al-Nour,

Chairman, Sudan Liberation Movement

ATTN: U.S. Special Envoy for Sudan and

South Sudan, Ambassador Donald Booth

Response by: Sudan Liberation Movement, Chairman, Abdul Wahid al-Nour to

November 22, 2016 *Sudan Tribune* opinion column on Darfur Crisis by US Ambassador and Special Envoy to Sudan and South Sudan, Donald Booth

Sir

Your calumnious editorial scapegoating me as the primary obstacle to peace in Darfur is so glaringly devoid of truth, morality or fairness that it becomes a caricature of itself, presenting so false a narrative. It does injury to the eye and history to read your slander but it is most of all blood libel to 600,000 dead Darfuris, the vast bulk of them civilians, killed in a deliberate genocide, under a state policy of ethnic cleansing, scorched earth, criminal neglect, death and torture endured by my people.

I, therefore, must personally condemn and repudiate your tragi-farcical communiqué in the harshest possible terms not only for its mendacity but ultimately for what verges on criminal incitement in encouraging the Sudanese regime to perpetrate more atrocities. That you issued your missive when incontrovertible evidence has emerged of Sudanese regime use of chemical weapons in Darfur, and you are silent on this point, eviscerates the honest broker persona you portrayed yourself as and leaves you ethically bereft.

Eight years ago, then presidential hopeful Barack Obama at least paid lip service to ending Darfur's suffering and expressed what seemed at the time, heartfelt empathy, just as George Bush Jr., had earlier first correctly decried the slaughter of my people as genocide but in this the new era of President-elect Trump, it seems the concept of "post-truth" also applies to the US State Department and you too Ambassador Booth in your cynical moral flexibility towards Sudan and Darfur in particular.

Never would I have imagined to see a senior US Diplomat publicly playing apologist for a hard line Islamist dictatorship linked to multiple terror groups, led by the sole sitting president on earth, Omar al-Bashir, indicted by the International Criminal Court for Crimes Against Humanity. It is a sinister page turning, Washington softly providing Khartoum carte blanche in an active genocide. You have done nothing less than this, de facto exculpated and legitimized ongoing state terrorism by Sudan against its own population.

Will you thus admit to the true purpose of your visible efforts to rehabilitate the regime, to which the fate of the Darfuri people is readily sacrificed, where we are subordinate and judged expendable to your aims?

Your bid to enlist Khartoum as an ally against Salafist extremism, while ignoring its own brutal authoritarianism, criminal conduct, enduring linkages and sponsorship of Islamist extremism is as myopically doomed to failure as US humanitarian policy on Darfur is self-evidently, a hollow and un-kept promise, now only more flagrant a betrayal of the democratic principles you avow to defend, you have traded for the expedient Realpolitik you're peddling.

You've not only conflated the victim with the victimizer, you have placed us in reverse categories, where those under the bombs are cast as villains and those that drop them are reasonable. The Dystopia is not of our making; it is yours.

You present me as the principal obstacle to peace, as though I were inexplicably and irrationally stubborn in rejecting what is ostensibly, sincere, government peace overtures. You paint me further as someone removed from the struggle of his people, as an aloof figure, suggesting subtly that I have somehow also lost the pulse of my people, as if you knew them better and can more readily speak to their aspirations, heartbreak or indignation than I or the Sudan Liberation Movement can? Shall we walk together in one of the Displaced People' s camps or clamber to a cliff top position to visit SLM fighters or speak to those sheltering from the bombs in the caves? I will show you then if my people still recognize me but I doubt they will have kind words for you.

I live and breathe only to deliver my people from the hell they daily endure to grant them a brighter, more just future where they may live in peace and security. To do so there is no aspect of my existence that isn't consecrated to this cause. I was born on the soil of Darfur. I bear wounds borne in battle for defending Darfur. My life belongs to Darfur, if needs be, my death too. How dare you attempt to judge me or my people, when you do not inhabit our skin or our condition? Yours is the worst possible, faux paternalism and we discard it as a matter of principle for it has the whiff of neo-colonialism. We do not fight because we relish it. We are weary of war and fight only because we are left with no equitable or palatable alternatives. We fight for sheer survival to save ourselves from extermination. We fight alone, largely unheard, unseen, a forgotten, disposable people.

Please elucidate Ambassador Booth how it is possible to enter into a peace dialogue or negotiations in good faith when the relentless brutalization of my people is unceasing? Disingenuously, you admit at the end of your bizarre missive that I may have cause to distrust the regime for over a decade of genocidal violence against my people. Better to have presented this key truth at the outset of any discourse concerning myself or the SLM's refusal to engage in the travesty of a peace dialogue with Khartoum, which has never shown itself to be sincere. A priori my actions and those of the SLM are belligerent, precisely because the regime has to date never abandoned the violent subjugation to my people. We find it distinctly difficult to speak when we are routinely, shot, shelled, bombarded, gassed, tortured or raped.

Even as I write you now, government troops, their partner militias and death squads do their worst in Darfur, South Kordofan and Blue Nile State.

Negotiations by Khartoum are illusory; they serve only to grant the regime greater leverage in seemingly appearing amenable to dialogue, while the guns continue to speak for the regime, its true language. So long as this remains practice, the SLM will not participate and will continue to boycott any such overtures by Khartoum.

We will happily confine our fighters to their base camps and observe a cessation of hostilities, if the regime withdraws it's soldiers and paramilitaries from civilian population centers, if it ceases the practice of extra-judicial summary executions, the use of torture, rape en masse and pledges to never make use of chemical weapons again and submits it's chemical weapons stockpiles to international inspection for disposal.

The notion that the SLM impedes joint AU-UN so called peacekeeping force access to investigate government atrocities is as ludicrous a premise as stating that the SLM blocks access to humanitarian supplies, when the SLM has begged the international community to end the crippling embargo on essential supplies, which the regime uses as a tool of war to better enable disease and hunger.

Just as the SLM will continue to call for free and open access to the media and human rights investigators, it will also demand a new international force to more ably carry out its duty in Darfur, where it is long overdue to accept that the combined peacekeeping mission in Darfur is an abject failure. The people of Darfur would be thrilled if the blue helmets would actually protect them, but when the mission is starved of the necessary manpower, resources, lacking in a sorely needed peace enforcement mandate, decisive leadership and repeatedly shown itself willing to be Khartoum' s pawn, our hopes are not high.

What truly beggars believe is that you contradict your own experience. Not long ago you met with civil leaders in three IDPs camps, all relaying their omnipresent fears of being attacked, disappeared, tortured or killed by government backed militias, paramilitaries, soldiers or police. You guaranteed their safety for openly meeting with you. All of them were later arrested and their fates as yet remain unknown and are unlikely to have been kind. How has this slipped your memory? We fight for a secular, free and pluralist, democratic Sudan, where sectarian violence and zealotry of every variety, in particular religious, racial or tribal chauvinism and ideological extremism of every stripe will no longer be state policy. We wish for all Sudanese to live in peaceful coexistence, tolerance and equanimity and we do draw partial inspiration from your Civil Rights Movement, your rule of law, democratic process and the unmatched diversity of your civil society.

Ambassador Booth, the people of Darfur will have Abdul Wahid at the negotiating table, when it is just and reasonable for me to occupy such a seat, with the confidence that the human rights, civil rights and dignity of my people and their right to live will not be casually violated as I do so. Self-defense is our God given right as is freedom from willful stupidity.

We will not sacrifice needlessly when we already die in droves. When the Sudanese regime has shown itself able only to mete out death and destruction, as it duplicitously spoke of peace, your entirely fictive rendition of the reality of Sudan and Darfur will have no bearing on the actions of the SLM. As it is, your manipulative, counter-intuitive and cynical reproach, casts serious doubts about your commitment to the well being of the people of Darfur and your truer intentions. As we refuse to become your distorted and utterly false narrative. Americans do not seem to hold answers for Darfur any longer, not that they ever did.

Sincerely,   Abdul Wahid Al-Nour, Chairman, Sudan Liberation Movement

Chapter Three
Obama's Folly: Executive Order No. 13761
lifting Sudan Sanctions

President Barack Obama signs Executive Order No. 13761

Background

Virtually one week before the inauguration of President Trump, President Barack Obama issued Executive Order No. 13761, "Recognizing Positive Actions by the Government of Sudan and Providing for the Revocation of Certain Sudan-Related Sanctions" temporarily lifting 20 years of sanctions against the Muslim Brotherhood National Congress Party (NCP) regime of President Omar Ahmad Hassan al-Bashir. He had been indicted for crimes against humanity by the International Criminal Court (ICC) at The Hague in 2009 and 2010.

Those indictments resulting from UN independent investigations revealed Bashir and co-indicters of the NCP regime perpetration of genocide against indigenous black African peoples in Darfur, Nuba Mountains and the Blue Nile State. Bashir has an outstanding Red Tag arrest warrant requiring his arrest should he visit any countries that are signatories of the Treaty of Rome establishing the ICC. In one notorious example, he was not arrested by the Republic of South Africa in 2015, when he attended the African Union Conference.

President Obama's rationale was alleged recent improvement in the so-called 'five tracks' of monitoring Sudan's behavior. His declaration stated:

> *I, Barack Obama,* President of the United States of America, find that the situation that gave rise to the actions taken in Executive Order 13067 of November 3, 1997, and Executive Order 13412 of October 13, 2006, related to the policies and actions of the Government of Sudan has been altered by Sudan's positive actions over the past 6 months. These actions include a marked reduction in offensive military activity, culminating in a pledge to maintain a cessation of hostilities in conflict areas in Sudan, and steps toward the improvement of humanitarian access throughout Sudan, as well as cooperation with the United States on addressing regional conflicts and the threat of terrorism.

He left it up to his successor, President Donald Trump to make a final determination by July 12, 2017 in accordance with the criteria set forth in President Obama's executive order.

Controversy immediately surrounded the issuance of President Obama's Executive order 13761.

The move by the Obama administration was "welcomed" by the Arab League in a *Qatar Tribune* report. This was a dramatic 'sea change' from a President Obama who campaigned during his 2008 election on "ending the slaughter in Darfur."

Outgoing US UN Ambassador Samantha Power rationalized the lifting of economic sanctions, imposed since 1997, at her farewell press conference, saying there was "progress on counterterrorism and cease fires." She attributed 'progress' on counterterrorism to Sudan ending its harboring of the murderous child soldier movement of the Lord's Resistance Army (LRA) of Joseph Kony. All while evidence mounted in reports of New Year's attacks by the Bashir regime's Jihadist militia in Darfur, the Nuba Mountains and Blue Nile region. These actions breached cease fires, threatening a renewal of ethnic cleansing of indigenous peoples and fomenting monumental humanitarian crises.

Veteran Sudan genocide watcher, Eric Reeves in a *Huffington Post* article called the Obama Administration executive order, "The Final Betrayal of Sudan". He focused on the current humanitarian crisis in Darfur and especially in the Blue Nile region. The Obama administration's Sudan sanctions action was "upsetting" to Kutum

Sudan Police torturing Darfurian Women, Kutum, Sudan

Mark Brand of Jewish World Watch in a *The Hill* op Ed. *The Wall Street Journal* reported criticism of the Obama Administration decision as "inexplicable" from Leslie Lefkow, deputy Africa director at Human Rights Watch. House Foreign Affairs, Chairman, Rep. Ed Royce (R-California) characterized it as a "last ditch effort, urging the new administration to look at Sudan with fresh eyes."

This last minute rapprochement with Jihadist Sudan by the former Obama Administration came in the face of a warning issued by Trump Adviser Dr. Walid Phares. He spoke at a Washington, DC conference with Nuba Mountain Sudan émigrés just after the election of President Trump on November 11, 2016. He avowed, "There is no reason for why we and our European allies should be lifting these sanctions, this is unacceptable. Lifting the sanctions on Bashir's regime is not acceptable". Yet, the Wall Street Journal reported that senior officials from the Obama Administration said that the Trump transition team had been briefed on the changes.

US Rep. Jim McGovern, (D) Mass., arrested at Sudan Embassy protest
March 16, 2012

Criticism of the bi-Partisan Congressional Human Rights Caucus

When President Obama announced his lifting of sanctions against Sudan, Democrat Massachusetts Congressman Jim McGovern, co-chair of the bi-partisan Congressional Tom Lantos Human Rights Commission responded with this scathing statement on January 13, 2017:

> I am angry and deeply disappointed that the last act by the Obama Administration on Sudan policy is to ease sanctions against a genocidal regime when there has been little to no change on the ground in the human rights and humanitarian crises suffered by the Sudanese people.

> Let us make no mistake: Sudanese President Omar al-Bashir is a war criminal. He and his brutal, corrupt cronies have been indicted for acts of genocide, crimes against humanity and war crimes. Any kind of sanctions relief should only have happened after the humanitarian and human rights situation had markedly changed on the ground.

> Khartoum remains a brutal authoritarian government that represses its own people, cracks down on democratic dissent and political opposition, provides no space for a free and independent press, and has yet to allow the delivery of desperately needed humanitarian aid to the suffering people of Darfur, South Kordofan and Blue Nile.

For me, the bottom line is whether the genocidal policies and practices of the Bashir government have changed. In my opinion, they have not. Women and children, the young and the old, are dying from slow starvation due to Khartoum's scorched earth military campaigns and the denial of humanitarian aid to those in need. Until such time as unimpeded access by international and humanitarian relief groups is happening and aid is actually being delivered to those in need, I remain skeptical that any such good will gestures by our government are warranted.

McGovern prodded the incoming Trump Administration to act, saying:

As for the process that has just been put in place, I ask that the incoming Trump Administration make sure that conditions have truly changed on-the-ground when making its determination in six months whether to make today's temporary relief permanent, let alone expanded. There can be no backsliding and there must be concrete change in the reality of the most besieged regions. Truly, people's very lives are at stake.

Congressman McGovern has demonstrated his resolute commitment to Sudan freedom. He has been arrested three times for chaining himself to the entrance of the Sudan Embassy in Washington. In a May 2016, letter to former President Obama co-signed by 120 Members of Congress demanding that the US keep the humanitarian crisis in the Sudan as a high priority, McGovern wrote:

As the violence in Sudan grows worse, the world is looking to the United States to be a strong partner in the effort to build a lasting peace and address this devastating humanitarian crisis. Today in Sudan, families are being displaced, hunger and malnutrition have reached crisis levels, and civilians face the constant threat of aerial bombings. With today's letter, our bipartisan coalition is calling on President Obama to make Sudan a top priority by taking new steps to protect the Sudanese people and put an end to this violent conflict.

Clearly, former President Obama chose for whatever reasons to dismiss the concern of McGovern and colleagues in the House. Instead he rewarded indicted war criminal President Bashir by lifting 20-year old US sanctions, for allegedly helping to locate the elusive head of the Lord's Resistance Army, Joseph Kony. In fact, one of the co-authors, Gen. Abakar M. Abdallah had provided GPS coordinates on Kony's location to the USAFRICOM, which never confirmed recognition. According to a report from *The WarZone:*

Special Operations Command (Forward)-Central Africa—aka SOCFWD-CA—coordinates operations, including contractor-flown cargo planes and helicopters and manned intelligence-gathering aircraft, out of Entebbe International Airport, in Uganda. As part of the mission, American special operators and their partners have access to small airstrips in Obo in the Central African Republic, Dungu in the Democratic Republic of Congo, and Nzara in South Sudan.

Congressman McGovern was cited in a March 3, 2017 *Sudan Tribune* report saying:

> This week, Jim McGovern, a senior House Democrat and leading voice in Congress on human rights, met with the Speaker of the Sudanese Parliament Ibrahim Ahmed Omer.
>
> In a press release on Tuesday, the Democratic Co-Chair of the Tom Lantos Human Rights Commission said during the meeting that Sudan's National Assembly and Omer in particular, "have been responsible for authorizing many of the most repressive actions carried out by the regime of President Bashir".
>
> "And therefore are accountable for the murder of millions of their fellow citizens and for the humanitarian crisis in Sudan," he added.
>
> According to the press release, the Congressman "plans to reintroduce bipartisan legislation this year to impose targeted sanctions on the Sudanese government for its genocidal acts and crimes against humanity".
>
> McGovern insisted "on the continuing need for unfettered humanitarian access, the release of all political prisoners and the cessation of all hostilities" in order to further improve bilateral relationship between the U.S. and Sudan.
>
> He accused the Sudanese government of renewing attacks against the Sudan People's Liberation Movement/North (SPLM-N) positions in South Kordofan and the Blue Nile.
>
> "Rather than ensure humanitarian access to South Kordofan, Darfur and Blue Nile, Khartoum has renewed offensive operations in South Kordofan, in violation of the agreements reached with the Obama Administration that resulted in the easing of sanctions," he pointed out.
>
> South Kordofan and neighboring Blue Nile states has been the scene of violent conflict between the SPLM-N and Sudanese army since 2011.
>
> Last August, the two sides failed to reach a humanitarian cessation of hostilities deal paving the way for political talks including the political opposition parties.

The *Sudan Tribune* noted US diplomat Koutsis' renewal of an offer of aid by the USAID:

> In an opinion article published in *Sudan Tribune* on March 3, 2017 Koutsis reiterated the U.S. proposal saying Washington has offered to deliver humanitarian medical assistance to the people in the SPLM-N controlled areas.
>
> "Our offer to oversee and implement these deliveries intends to give confidence to the SPLM-N that the Government of Sudan would not be able to control or block aid provided under this mechanism," said Koutsis.
>
> He pointed out that the Sudanese government "has agreed to this proposal, but as of yet, the SPLM-N has not allowed the proposal for humanitarian access to go forward".
>
> "Given current predictions of emergency-level food insecurity likely to occur within the next two months in SPLM-N controlled areas, an agreement to allow humanitarian access to begin now is critical to save lives," he warned.
>
> "The United States urges the SPLM-N to remove political conditions preventing humanitarian assistance from reaching populations in need and allow rapid deployment of humanitarian aid to civilians in the areas it controls," he further said.

Co-author, Deborah Martin, when she was in South Sudan in March 2017 had spoken to the SPLA-N high command who disputed these statements from former US Special Envoy to Sudan, Donald Booth, and US Charge d'affaires, Koutsis. SPLA-N officials contend they have not rejected humanitarian aid. Rather, it was the opposite; they were asking for coordination of humanitarian aid deliveries with USAID or other agencies, but not through Khartoum. Both Booth and Koutsis may have 'misinterpreted' the SPLA-N offer of co-ordination as rejection. In either case, the US officials sent the wrong message to both regional and international communities.

Evidence of Continuing Jihad in Darfur and Adjacent Sahel areas

According to Sudan United Movement Chairman and co-author, Gen. Abdallah, there was fresh evidence of continuing Jihad by the Orwellian named 'Peace Force' of President Bashir in Darfur and neighboring the Central African Republic.

The Sortini Internally Displaced Persons (IDP) camp has been under siege for nearly a year. The Janjaweed 'Peace Force' militias established roadblocks around the camp, in July 2016, preventing anyone from leaving the camp to the nearby town of Kapkabiya in north Darfur. *Radio Dabanga News* reported in January 2017 that nine women had been systematically raped. Men and young boys could not go out of the camp to fetch firewood and water without being in danger of being shot and killed. The 'Peace Force' militias burned down their villages destroyed their farms and fruit plantations, while they were under siege in full view of the international community. UNAMID forces cannot leave the IDP camp to protect women and young girls collecting firewood or fetching water by order of Khartoum. The only access to the camp is by air. These IDP victims were removed from their land by force. Men are systematically killed and women are systematically raped, terrorizing this vulnerable population. They have been forced to abandon their land to Arab Janjaweed 'Peace Force' militias. A veritable jihad army of more than 150,000 foreign terrorists from adjacent lands in the Sahel and the Middle East were brought by the Bashir regime and trained, equipped and deployed from at least 16 camps in the Khartoum region.

When co-author, Deborah Martin, interviewed members of the Sudan Peoples Liberation Army-North [SPLA-N] for the Nuba Mountains and Blue Nile region, they confirmed capture of Jihadists from Niger, Mali, Libya and ISIS trained in the 16 camps in Khartoum.

President of The Republic of the Sudan, Omar al-Bashir- battle ready

The international community had stood by while the Sudan regime of indicted war criminal President Bashir has pursued a strategy outlined in a Secret Arab Coalition document uncovered in 2014 by General Abdallah. (See Chapter Five "Revealed: Bashir's Secret Jihad Plan for Sudan"). The objective of the captured Arab Coalition Plan is to entirely eradicate the indigenous population of African origin by 2020 replacing them with Arab tribes. The Bashir regime has plans to bring them from neighboring countries, such as Quran living in Northern Chad, and settling them in the area of Disah, North Darfur. The Bashir regime's new strategy for the fighting season in 2017 is to form an alliance with the Quran tribe in the Northern parts of Chad and settle them in Darfur. The regime has displaced indigenous Darfurians into 150 IDP camps inside the region and 12 UN refugee camps in Chad. On their arrival, these settlers from Chad are provided with arms and integrated into the 'Peace Force' Janjaweed militia controlled by the regime National Intelligence and Security Service.

The humanitarian cease fire declared on January 13, 2017, when former President Obama lifted sanctions against the Bashir regime in Khartoum, was breached on February 21, 2017 and was reported by the SPLA-N:

> The Sudanese army and its allied militia started their dry season offensive at 6AM at Krongos Abdalah in Kadugli County, breaching the declared joint cease fire. This came after a well orchestrated political campaign and hate speech against the SPLM-N and the Nuba people. We will repulse the offensive and call upon the regional and international community to condemn this offensive and hold the Sudan government responsible. The area is heavily inhabited by civilian population. We warned the Sudanese government from using their air force against the civilian population, which they usually do.

The loss of an important US Intelligence asset on Africa: Robin Townley

Another controversy erupted in February 2017 over the resignation of President Trump's appointment of former Defense Intelligence Agency (DIA) director, Lt. Gen. Michael T. Flynn as National Security Adviser over alleged Russian collusion during the 2016 President Election campaign. One of Flynn's appointments to the National Security was a former US Marine Intelligence officer, Robin Townley who had served with General Flynn during the second Iraq War. Townley had also served under Flynn during the General's term at DIA and had conducted a series of reconnaissance missions in the Northern and Central African conflict zones. A February 13, 2013 *intellNews* report noted that Townley, who had been appointed by Flynn as Senior Director for Africa, had been asked to step down, given objections by the Central Intelligence Agency regarding that Townley was ineligible to receive a Special Compartmentalized Intelligence Facility clearance for access to highly sensitive information. *IntellNews* reported, " Townley was considered 'one of Flynn's closest deputies', held a top-secret security clearance for many years during his government career." Apparently, Townley's resignation had been approved by President

Trump's CIA director appointment, former Kansas Republican Congressman, Mike Pompeo.

Townley's departure from the Trump National Security Council in retrospect may have been a real loss for Sudan resistance commanders and also for informed assessment of any improvement by the Sudan regime of President Bashir under the Obama Executive Order No. 13761.

Conclusion

The Trump Administration should support Congressman McGovern's call for rescinding the Obama Administration lifting of sanctions against the Bashir regime in the Sudan. This could be achieved by executive order or legislation as proposed by the bi-partisan Congressional Human Rights Commission. In support of such executive and legislative actions, testimony was subsequently submitted to the US House Subcommittee on Africa and Global Terrorism chaired by New Jersey Republican Congressman, Chris Smith by the Darfurian Sudan United Movement, SPLA-N senior resistance commanders and SPLM-N political leaders. That testimony presented the compelling facts on the ground about Genocidal Jihad perpetrated by the regime of indicted war criminal Bashir. Further, it explored both political and military options for facilitating the ultimate solution of regime change and political settlement of this flagrant humanitarian crisis. (See Chapter Nine)

Chapter Four
President Bashir's "Peace Force" perpetrates Jihad.

Evidence of Bashir's Continuing Jihad in Darfur

The New Year, 2017, brought dramatic evidence of Bashir's Jihad strategy. A massacre occurred in the Central Darfur town of Nertiti by marauding Sudan Armed Forces and 'Peace Forces' mercenaries killing 11, injuring 60 civilians.

This massacre demonstrated Bashir's callous intent, when he had declared a "cease fire" with resistance forces. On January 5, 2017 'Peace Forces' militias attacked people in Hay al Jebel in Geneina killing 7 people and wounding 16 others. The Geneina massacre occurred following the end of the visit of Sudan's 2nd Vice President Hassabo Mohamed Abderhaman who spent two weeks in Geneina. Since January 2016, he frequently moved between Southern, Central and Western Darfur regions mobilizing Arab recruits from Chad and the Central African Republic (CAR) for the Sudan 'Peace Forces'.

The reality is that Sudan President Bashir has mobilized and equipped an international Jihad army of over 150,000 from across the Sahel region and Syria to make the final push for ethnic cleaning in Darfur, the Nuba Mountains and the

Blue Nile Region. Not unlike The Lord's Resistance Army, the Janjaweed militias, now renamed 'Peace Forces,' continue to actively recruit child soldiers aged 8 to 12 years. Sudan's indicted war criminal President Omar Bashir called on the international community to support his false peace process in Sudan.

Peace Force militias massacre of civilians on January 5, 2017 in Geneina

Contrary to the promise he made to the people of America during his campaign to put an end to genocide in Darfur; Obama's Administration closely cooperated with the genocidal regime in the name of combating terrorism. Cooperation with Khartoum's regime helped Bashir to continue committing genocide against the people of Darfur and to create more terrorist organizations in the world. By signing this executive order, President Obama betrayed the oppressed people of Darfur. Without Obama's support Bashir could not continually have committed genocide against the people of Darfur, since his two International Criminal Court indictments in 2009 and 2010.

Hoping to obtain intelligence information to combat global terrorism, Obama's Administration systematically failed to reveal President Bashir and his Arab cabal's secret mobilization of Mujahideen militias known as Rapid Support Forces. The creation of these new forces would be in line with the regime's strategy of forming and adopting militias. Now the 'RSF' has been replaced with the Orwellian 'Peace Forces.' As the strategy of establishing the Caliphate in Africa has not yet been realized, we will doubtless continue to see a succession of new iterations to hide the real identity of Bashir's Jihadist army.

Nertiti, Central Darfur Sudan Peace Forces Casualties January 1, 2017

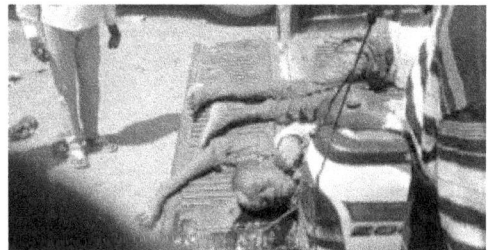

The question that one could ask is: on what grounds did President Obama base his facts that Bashir's regime had improved its human rights record in Darfur? This view of improvement persists despite the Nertiti and Geneina massacres by Bashir's 'Peace Forces' in January 2017.

What type of terrorism has the Obama's Administration been fighting, if President al-Bashir is currently mobilizing and recruiting Mujahideen in Jelly, North Darfur to join a multinational offensive?

What was the motivation behind the Obama Administration signed executive order that the genocidal regime of Bashir had reduced its human right abuses in Darfur?

New terrorist groups continually arrive in Darfur from Libya through Dongola, in North Sudan. These new groups are escorted to Darfur by 'Peace Forces' that some EU governments support technically and finance to allegedly combat illegal immigrant flow from Africa. These terrorist groups have reportedly been seen in Southern and Eastern Darfur regions. They are believed to include Boko Haram and ISIS jihadis. Villagers who have encountered them reported they are a mixture of Arabs and Africans. The latter look like Nigerians. Those who resemble Arabs or Egyptians do not speak Arabic. They communicate with people only through interpreters. They frequently ask the names of places, directions and distances. They also depend on the use of maps and GPS to travel. They possess ISIS flags and wear the Kodomul (black turban). They are moving on Toyota pickup trucks similar to those used by 'Peace Forces'. The Sudan regime pretends that these 'Peace Forces' are combating illegal immigrants. In reality, they are helping bring in terrorists and Chadian rebels from Libya to Darfur. With the mobilization of newly created 'Peace Forces' and the arrival of terrorist groups from Libya, Darfur war crimes will continue to go from bad to worse.

How the Peace Forces are recruited

Some Arabs of Darfur disagree with the government fearing for their future executing the regime's plan to use them against other tribes of Darfur. Others disputes arise because the government gave senior positions in the Peace Forces to these new arrivals. The government of the Sudan continues to organize Janjaweed militias into different forms but their mission is to create the Caliphate.

Peace Forces child soldier using arms

Each Arab sheik must bring 200 men to be recruited into the Peace Forces. Currently each sheik is required to bring 50 men. The remaining 150 must be recruited from both adults and children aged 8 and 12 years old. Each sheik is also authorized 10 military officers' ranks. What is strange is that two of these officers' ranks should be a full Colonel and the other a Lieutenant Colonel will be chosen by the government. The rest from Major down to 2nd Lieutenant will be selected by lottery.

The rest of 190 people will participate in a lottery game to determine who will be picked to be among the remaining eight officers. The rest will be enlisted personnel. If an eight year old kid pulled a Major's rank he will be confirmed as a Major in the Sudanese army and enjoy full status, but will not take command responsibility until he reaches a certain age. Normally, Janjaweed children as young as 8 years old can carry weapons. All these people will be paid salaries. Military ranks and salaries are made to encourage or compensate them on the work they are doing for the Caliphate. Recruiting an 8 to 12 year old child indicates that the Arab cabal is determined to establish a Caliphate in the Sahel Region of Africa. Darfur will be used as a base to execute this strategy.

Ethnic Cleansing in CAR

Ethnic cleansing has been going on in Bambari, Bria, and their surroundings in the Central African Republic (CAR). The fighting erupted between SELEKA groups. SELEKA split into several groups. Following the election of the new President of CAR, the government in Bangui tried to integrate SELEKA rebel forces into the CAR army, but some of these factions refused. A faction lead by the Ali Dressa majority from the Fulani tribe welcomed the government offer.

The rest of SELEKA factions are lead by tribes of Gula, Runga, and Arabs who rejected the offer. They are united against the Fulani faction. Fighting erupted between these groups and escalated into tribal conflicts. SELEKA lead by an Arab named Hakim received reinforcements of men and weapons from Janjaweed militias in Darfur and Arabs of Chad. We heard horrible stories of Fulani women carrying babies in their hands begging for their lives who were killed by machetes not for any reason but because they are Fulani. Fighting continues between SELEKA is believed to have been committed on all sides. The strategy of creating the Caliphate in the Sahel by the Bashir regime in Khartoum is

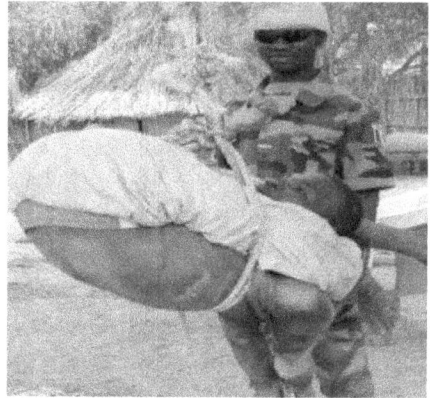

Chadian Rebel in Sudan with Darfur victim

moving faster than we had imagined. The Janjaweeds now control nearly half of CAR territory. They hold territory from Bambari in the center all the way to Sam bordering South Sudan and the areas bordering Southern Chad. The only hope is to separate Gulas and Rungas and unite them with Fulani to drive Janjaweed away from CAR.

President Bashir and his Arab allies' Islamic 'Peace Forces' have not stopped committing genocide, war crimes and crimes against the black indigenous people of Darfur. With the objective of furthering the Islamic extremist ideology,

Peace Force militias burning homes on Hay al Jebel in Geneina January 5, 2017

they have extended killing to the adjacent population, Central African Republic and Chad. This is all part of his plan to establish, through removal of African tribes, a Caliphate in the Sahel region of Central Africa. Meanwhile, tens of thousands of foreign Islamist terrorists and mujahideen from across Africa and Syria are gathering and being trained in 16 camps in the Sudan for the conducting of this Jihad.

Sudan's interior Minister admitted to the members of parliament on January 4, 2017 that there were over 3,000-armed foreign fighters present in Jebel Amir, Darfur. This was not the first time the Sudan government revealed that there were foreign fighters in Darfur. The fact is that these fighters were brought in by the regime and controlled by its security agents in order to expand a Jihadist army.

Conclusion

The international community, especially those countries that are embracing Bashir's regime, should take notice that the National Congress Party/Muslim Brotherhood regime in Khartoum poses a threat to international peace and security. Bashir's strategy of raising a veritable Jihadist army to establish a Caliphate in the African Sahel region is continuing. If his strategy and his allies are not stopped, it could destabilize the whole sub-region. The Trump Administration now has the opportunity to change course in the region by the appointment of a new independent minded Special Envoy in Sudan. That appointee should have special expertise on Islamic counterterrorism to monitor abuses by the Bashir regime in Darfur, the Nuba Mountains and Blue Nile Region. As the date of this writing the Trump administration has not appointed a Special Envoy in Sudan.

Chapter Five
Revealed: Bashir's secret Jihad plan for Sudan

President Bashir April 2016

In "Chapter Three," Obama Lifts Sudan Sanctions While President Bashir perpetrates Jihad, we reported on the lifting of 20 years of sanctions against the regime of President Omar al-Bashir for making progress against counterterrorism in the Sudan. All while he was preparing to launch a Jihad army of 150,000 recruited from across the Sahel region and the Middle East, including the Islamic State. Many of those jihadists were recruited from Islamic terrorist groups from Libya, neighboring Chad, the Central African Republic, Mali and Niger. They have been undergoing training in 16 camps around Khartoum. These cadres were composed of formations of Janjaweed/Rapid Support forces now renamed 'Peace Forces'. By early February 2017, the Bashir regime completed training of 34,000 'Peace Force' militia at the Kerere and Fatasha camps near Khartoum. 2,500 of these Peace Force militia, equipped with heavily armed militarized Hi-Lux Toyota pickup trucks, have been deployed at at the Jadeed al Sail training camp in the North Darfur capital of Fashir. Bashir's jihad army is already on the attack in Darfur.

To understand the Jihad doctrine behind Bashir's strategy we are presenting the underlying doctrinal strategy found in a captured secret document, the Arab

Coalition Guresh 1 and 2. Guresh is the name for the Prophet Mohammed's tribe in Arabia, used by the people for themselves.

The Arabic Language version of a Sudan Arab Coalition document of 11 pages was captured during the fighting between the Rapid Support Forces (RSF) (reorganized Janjaweed Militias) and Darfur rebels in October 2014 in Donky Hush, North Darfur. The document was found in an abandoned military truck belonging to the RSF. It was translated by Lt. General Abakar M. Abdallah, Chairman of the Sudan United Movement in April 2015 to document the genocidal Jihad doctrine underlying the ethnic cleansing of Darfur, the Nuba Mountains Blue Nile Region and South Kordofan.

The document, containing different Guresh statements of the Sudan Arab Coalition project, was created in 1987 by former Sudan Prime Minister Sadiq al-Mahdi who founded the Janjaweed militias. Al-Mahdi and the late Islamic reformer Dr. Hassan al-Turabi had drafted in the 1960's the Islamic manifesto to rule Sudan under Sharia Islamic law creating the Arabization and Islamization policies. Those policies are currently being implemented by his usurper, indicted war criminal President Omar al-Bashir. They form the core of the Jihad doctrine found in the Arab Coalition document.

Al-Mahdi is the great grandson of Muhammad Ahmad, who declared himself the Mahdi, "the guided one" in Arabic, who would rule until the Day of Judgment under Islamic doctrine. The Mahdi established a Sharia ruled Caliphate in the Sudan in 1881 directed at invading Egypt seeking to overturn the infidels, the Khedive Egyptian ruler and his British allies. The Mahdi's army conducted a siege at Khartoum resulting in its capture and the death of valiant British Major General, Sir Charles Gordon, in 1885. The Mahdi's Caliphate ended with the reconquest of the Sudan by a combined British - Egyptian force under General Sir Herbert Kitchener at the Battle of Omdurman on September 2, 1898 that defeated an army led by the Mahdi's successor Abdullah al-Taashi. The Sudan campaign was chronicled in Sir Winston Churchill's *The River War: An Account of the Reconquest of the Sudan*. The British subsequently reached a settlement with the Al-Mahdi family in 1910 bestowing on them a fortune of 110,000 pounds Sterling.

The Anglo-Egyptian Sudan established in 1902 ended with the declaration of the Republic of Sudan in 1956. Almost immediately a more than half century civil war broke out between the Arab north versus the indigenous African tribes in the South resulting in the creation of South Sudan as a new nation in 2011. Notwithstanding, the genocidal campaign, articulated in the Arab Coalition document, Jihad continued with open warfare against resistance forces in the Darfur, Nuba Mountains and Blue Nile region in South Kordofan.

Sadiq Al-Mahdi, an Oxford graduate, was overthrown in 1989 by then General now President Omar al-Bashir. Al-Mahdi went into exile for several purposes: 1) to gain credibility of opposition groups and militias; 2) to obtain popular support both in Sudan and externally; 3) to obtain support from Arab countries; 4) to eradicate armed rebellions to defend Arab supremacy in Sudan; and, 5) to rally opposition forces to weaken the regime. He returned in 2017 at the age of 80 to exploit current weaknesses of the Bashir regime seeking to replace it as the main Arab regime in Khartoum.

Objectives of the Arab Coalition Document

The Arab Coalition document carries forward the basic Jihad doctrine through the latest available edition in 2014. The central objective of the Arab Coalition document is to eradicate the people of Darfur and occupy the land by 2020. The most important part of this document is the evaluation of 2014 in which they distributed the entire Darfur region to different Arab tribes with the intention of completing their project by 2020. If the Arab Coalition plan is left unchecked by resistance forces, then Janjaweed militias will commit more genocidal atrocities in Darfur to complete their task.

The essential document declaring the creation of the Arab Assembly against Darfur was issued in March 1987. It was renewed following the evaluation of its advantages and disadvantages as well as the objectives that had been achieved in 1992. After 11 years, the implementation of the document was renewed in 2003. However, the objective of ethnic cleansing Darfur and other parts of Sudan was hampered by internal problems occurring between the Arab tribes: lack of adequate resources, the starting of rebellion in the Darfur region from non-Arab tribes, and the support of the international community to the Darfur cause. Sudan had been placed on the list of state sponsors of terrorism in 1993 by the US State Department. An indictment was issued in 2009 and 2010 by the International Criminal Court at The Hague directed against Sudan government officials accusing them of committing war crimes, crimes against humanity, and genocide in Darfur. Among those indicated were President Omar al-Bashir, Musa Hilal, Ahmed Haroun, and Ali Kosheeb.

Other problems emerged to prevent achievement of the Arab Coalition objectives. Some members diverted the funds collected for the purpose of executing this plan for personal benefits. Some tribes who initially agreed to support the project withdrew when they perceived that this project was not in their interests in the long term. They were effectively executing plans that at the end would eventually destroy them.

Note these objectives listed in the Arab Coalition document:

- Seize all livestock and resources from indigenous tribes;

- Kill their representatives, educated leaders and confine the rest of indigenous tribes in big cities, prisons, or kill them whenever there is an opportunity;
- Keep all government resources that can assist people on making complaints, or can be used in emergence cases, transportation, or communication so that they could not communicate between one another;
- Place camps of Arab fighters (Janjaweed) on high mountains so that the attackers cannot approach them; and
- Attack areas that have strong resistance with large forces.

According to the Arab Coalition document The Higher Committee of the Arab Assembly carried out the following tactical program to achieve jihad objectives:

- Create difficulties in the way of the regional governments and use all resources available so as not to be able to execute their policies and programs of development;
- Do everything possible to disrupt government services in the areas occupied by non-Arab tribes in order to make them feel the government weakness and its failure to provide necessary means for life;
- Increase the volunteers in areas occupied by non-Arab tribes to create insecurity problems, stop production and kill their leaders;
- Create disputes between non-Arab tribes to prevent unification.

The members of the Assembly occupying senior positions are obliged to do the following:

- Concentrate on providing services to the areas of the Arab Assembly;
- Do not employ non-Arabs in important positions;
- Create obstacles for those non-Arabs who occupy positions and work in administration;
- Try by all means to create instability in schools in non-Arab populated areas; and
- Whenever there is an opportunity kill them.

The projected timetable to achieve the Jihad war objectives in Darfur was six years from 2014 by which time the Arab Assembly was to finish the ' jihad project' in 2020. As the Arab Assembly had not been able by 2014 to execute the project, the Executive Committee divided the rest of the areas of the Darfur region. That would allow new comers to settle in and work fast to complete the project, meaning replacement of indigenous African tribes with Arab settlers.

You may read the translated Arab Coalition document in Appendix B.

Chapter Six
Political Islam in Sudan supported by Qatar, the UAE and Saudi Arabia

Her Highness Sheikha Mozah Bint Nasser of Qatar with Sudan President Omar Bashir Khartoum, Sudan March 12, 2017

The Political Islamic system in the Sudan, spearheaded by the National Congress Party [NCP] regime of President Bashir in Sudan, is supported by the State of Qatar. The relationship contributes to growing Islamic extremist groups and international terrorism in the world. Some Salafi movement leaders in Khartoum openly support ISIS; some Sudanese college students are already fighting for Jihad in Libya and Syria. Sudan's geographical location and the ruling elite's historical ties with Middle East nations has been the main reason allowing the Khartoum regime to support global extremism in both ideology and fighting for Jihad without being stopped.

Those countries fighting in the global war against terrorism and the Islamic State failed to understand how Sudan's Muslim Brotherhood/National Congress Party (NCP) regime functions. The regime is telling the international community one thing and doing something else. For instance, the four Sudanese who killed John Granville, the American who was working in the USAID in Khartoum and his Sudanese driver, Abdelrhaman Abass, in 2008 were convicted to life sentences. However, the Sudan regime declared that they had escaped from prison. These men were convicted to deceive the American government that the Sudan regime was not behind the assassination. The regime convicted the men to mislead both the US government authorities and the victims' families that justice had been done. In reality, the Sudan regime released the prisoners under the pretext that they escaped from prison and sent them to fight as part of al Qaeda in Somalia and later to join the Islamic State and fight for ISIS in Libya.

A rise of Islamic movements in Sudan started in early 1930s. The Sudanese society is characterized by a geographic diversity reflected in its multi-cultural, multi-ethnic, multi-lingual and multi-religious populations. However, the Islamic movements ignored these facts and formed a government based on its ideology on sectarian parties, tribalism, and religious extremism that excluded the majority of the Sudan's population from their basic rights of citizenship. This exclusion has caused Sudan's perpetual crisis that resulted in an endless civil war that subjugated the population of the country.

Throughout the history of Sudan, the successive regimes have been using the same vicious slogans: "Sudan is an Arab land, Defending Islam, Spreading Islam in Africa, Defending the Palestine Cause, and Defending Arabism." Using these themes, successive regimes ruling Sudan were able to convince and at times mislead the Middle East nations to secure political, moral, material, and financial support.

It is in the context of this strategy that the NCP regime in Khartoum obtained financial support from Gulf States, because they ignored the majority non-Arab Sudanese people, seeing the Sudan as an Arab country; constructing an Islamic Arab state and defending the Arab cause against Africanism, imperialism (America), and Zionism (State of Israel). Such beliefs are an important part of their political, religious, and social cohesion that generates funding to finance all forms of terrorism not only in the Sudan, but also in the African Sahel region and the world. Those countries combating the global war on terrorism should understand these facts. They should deal with Bashir's regime committing genocidal war crimes and crimes against humanity against the people of Darfur, Blue Nile and Cordovan.

The NCP regime's ultimate goal is not to bring peace, stability, justice and the rule of law. Rather, it is to spread radical Islamic ideology eventually establishing a Caliphate in the Sudan at the expense of destroying the entire population in the country's conflict regions through the use of violence to intimidate its opponents. This regime has the habit of forming false alliances to resolve most crises. It also uses racial, ethnic, and tribalism to divide the people and deal with each group separately. The NCP government also uses religion as the word of God to frighten and control people. It uses deception, fomenting and financing of tribal conflicts, use of propaganda through its controlled media, forming alliances with under privileged groups. It uses state funds to bribe opponents to obtain their support consequently weakening them prior to their destruction. The NCP has not limited itself to the use of these tactics. It has also created Islamic institutions that function within and outside its government to advance its Islamic extremist ideological vision in the world. These organizations include but not limited to:

-**Leadership Bureau of the National Congress Party**. This is where all the powers of the NCP reside. All higher decisions emanate from this office. For example, appointment of executive positions such as ministers, ambassadors, governors, senior military commanders.

-**Islamic Movement (IM)**. The IM was created to serve as a political base for the NCP. IM unites domestic and international radical Islamist groups under its umbrella. It provides them with ideological guidance seeking to apply Islamic Sharia law to the **entire world**.

-**Islamic Da'wa Organization (IDO)**. The IDO is a Sudanese Islamic NGO founded in 1992 and designated to work in Africa. The organization is supported and funded by Saudi Arabia and other Arab Gulf States. IDO is a member of the International Islamic Council for Da'wa and Relief (IICDR). The IICDR is an umbrella of over 100 Islamic organizations most of them associated with Muslim Brotherhood, Al Qaeda, and Hamas. These organizations provide political guidance, ideology, recruitment, and funding for all Islamic Salafi movements in the world. IDO is headed by retired Field Marshal and former President of the Sudan Abderhaman Siwar al Dhahab. He is also the current Chairman of the Board of Trustees of the Union of Good (UOG) member organization. The UOG is designated by the US Department of the Treasury as a terrorist organization providing financial assistance to Hamas.

-**International University of Africa (IUA)**. The IUA is a public university located in Khartoum and like any other educational institution, has many faculties. However, it concentrates on two subjects: (1) Islamic Sharia and (2) Islamic studies. This institution is designed to train preachers and educate young African Muslims indoctrinating them with the Salafist view of Islam. The IUA University becomes an important Islamic center for Sub-Saharan Africa educating people in Islamic extremist ideology.

Through these organizations the Sudan government and Gulf States are engaged in spreading extremist Islamic ideology contributing to global extremism. If we look back a few years back, we saw that al Qaeda was present only in small areas of Afghanistan and Pakistan. Today, we see Jihads all over the world and they are developing rapidly. We are regularly receiving information that Sudan and Qatar are providing financial and military assistance to Islamic militants in Libya, Mali, and possibly to Boko Haram in Nigeria.

Despite US Government placing financial restrictions on Sudan, the Saudi Arabian government regularly donates money to the Sudan regime. Saudi Arabia gave Sudan $1billion in July and August 2015. These funds were given in the form of loans or investments. The Sudanese authorities mentioned that they expect to receive $4 billion following Khartoum's decision to join the Saudi-led military coalition against Houthi rebels in Yemen. The flow of money from Saudi Arabia to the Muslim Brotherhood regime in the Sudan contributes to financing Global Jihad.

The IM, IDO, IICDR, and UOG organizations collect funds not only from the oil rich Gulf States but also from companies, businessmen, Princes, Sheiks, traders, and ordinary people. These donations were not for the purpose of supporting terrorism, but for the goal of either advancing Pan-Arabism or supporting Islam. Most of these people do not care about the results of their donations. They assume it is for the purpose of advancing Islam or Arabism.

Sudan President Omar al-Bashir's 2015 state visit to South Africa, in violation of the outstanding International Criminal Court warrant for his arrest, was settled by the Emir of Dubai. He paid one hundred million dollars to the South African government within the week following the incident. The Emir travelled to South Africa and settled the deal. Why did the Emir pay this money? The Emir paid the money simply because he has business interest in Sudan and was defending Pan Arabism.

Her Highness Sheikha Mozah Bint Nasser, royal consort of Emir of Qatar Sheikh Hamad bin Khalifa Al Thani, visited Sudan on March 12, 2017. She was welcomed by the first lady of Sudan, Widad Babiker. She met with President Bashir and discussed development projects for Sudan. The Sheikha, also, visited North Kordofan State to meet with the notorious Janjaweed leader Ahmed Harun who has also been indicted by the International Criminal Court, but is still at large. In order to draw away the international community's attention Sheikha Mozah visited pyramids in Merowe, Sudan's historic city in which Qatar and Sudan have joint Archeological projects.

The Sudan government obtains funding from the Arab League and the oil rich Gulf Emirates through official and nonofficial channels. In 2007 and 2008, the Arab League gave the Sudan government over $500 million in the name of development in Darfur. Sheikha Mozah, who visited Khartoum on March 12, 2017, donated $200 million dollars to Bashir to recruit and train more Janjaweed militias. These funds will be used to finance terrorists and recruit

Janjaweed to kill the indigenous people of Darfur, Blue Nile and Kordofan. Even though the money came in the name of development. The wealthy oil rich Gulf Emirates, especially Qatar, provide Sudan funding in the name of development projects while secretly working to establish an all Arab Caliphate in Darfur and African Sahel region.

Following the visit of the Qatari State Minister in Darfur, he promised to fund 17 development projects in Darfur. Since the signing of the Darfur Doha agreement both Qatar and Sudan spoke of developments in Darfur. In July 2016, Chairman Tijani Sisi of the Darfur Regional Authority mentioned that his organization realized 1800 projects in Darfur. The fact is that over 3 million people of Darfur are living in internally displaced persons (IDPs) and UN High Commissioner Refugee camps in adjacent Chad. Where are the 1800 projects that Chairman Sisi was talking of that he and his group realized? Where is this large number of projects that could not be seen in Darfur? The truth is that there are no projects in Darfur other than recruiting and training of Janjaweed and terrorists to kill innocent people

The fact is that the Sudan government recruited and trained 34,000 Arab Janjaweed militias funded by State of Qatar. These Arab tribal militias are currently prepared to secure new settlement projects (construction of villages and digging of water pumps for new Arab settlers) in North Darfur. About the time of the Qatari Royal Personage visit to Khartoum in March 2017, the Bashir regime deployed over 100-armed Toyota Pickup trucks of Rapid Support Forces to provide security protection to dig these water pumps at Wadi Azerk in Wadi Hawar, North Darfur. Their plan was to create 1,200 new Janjaweed villages in the area north of Kutum adjacent to the borders of Libya. Villagers, in Disah, North Darfur, were told to abandon their villages and move to the IDP camps or to the cities because next year they will not be allowed to cultivate their land. They said that area north of Kutum to the border of Libya is designated for Arab Janjaweed animal husbandry.

Sheikha Mozah with innocent school children of North Kordofan
March 13, 2017

Conclusions

The Sudan government is contributing to the growing global Islamic extremist ideology and Jihadism. Eliminating this regime is a necessary requirement for peace. Its removal from Khartoum would greatly reduce the phenomenon of Islamic terrorism in the world. This would eliminate the system of sectarian parties, tribalism, and religious discrimination that successive regimes use to divide and rule Sudanese society. Regime change in Khartoum would call for creation of a secular and Sudanese identity transcending tribal and religious boundaries emphasizing equality and justice for its entire people.

Chapter Seven
Billions for Bashir at Arab League Summit

Sudan President al-Bashir with King Salman of Saudi Arabia, host King Abdullah II of Jordan and other leaders at the 2017 Amman Arab League meetings, March 29-30, 2017

Sudan President al-Bashir with King Salman of Saudi Arabia, host King Abdullah II of Jordan and other leaders at the 2017 Amman Arab League meetings, March 29-30, 2017

The Arab League Summit hosted by King Abdullah II of Jordan, March 29-30, 2017 at a resort near the Dead Sea, had more to report in its several declarations than rekindling peace talks between Israel and the Palestinians based on the 2002 plan of the late Saudi King Abdullah. Virtually unnoticed were reports of a wide-ranging series of economic development projects involving the members of the Gulf Cooperation Council, the Kingdom of Saudi Arabia and Emeriti players focused on the Sudan, hence the presence of indicted war criminal President Bashir.

The objective is to transform the Sudan into the virtual breadbasket for the Sunni Arab confederation in the Middle East. This economic integration plan would imply support for the strategic goal of the Khartoum regime's Arab Coalition plan for the Sudan that President Bashir hopes to conclude by 2020.

That plan's objective is the ethnic cleansing of indigenous people in Darfur, Nuba Mountains, South Kordofan and the Blue Nile Region with replacement by Arab tribal settlers from the Janjaweed Peace Force and foreign Jihadi fighters.

Tens of billions of dollars of Saudi and Emeriti funded projects were announced at the Arab League Summit providing the economic incentives for fulfillment of Bashir's Jihad and Caliphate plans for the Sudan and ultimately the Sahel region. This upwelling of Sunni Arab support for the Sudan followed President al-Bashir's switch of alliance in 2014 from the Shiite Islamic Republic of Iran.

What occurred at the Arab League Summit in Jordan?

A little noticed Arab news release on March 30, 2017, spelled out the deepening extent of the Sudan economic development projects on the agenda of the GCC members led by Saudi Arabia's King Salman. A translation revealed the following.

President Bashir visits Saudi King Salman Riyadh November 2015

King Salman bin Abdul Aziz at the Amman Arab League summit this year asked to be seated next to Sudan President Omar al-Bashir. The king extended an invitation to President al-Bashir to lunch at the residence of the Custodian of the Two Holy Mosques.

The Custodian of the Two Holy Mosques announced his intention to visit Khartoum in May 2018 to discuss the establishment of the largest integrated meat complex in the Middle East with a production capacity of 25 million heads of cattle per year.

Also on the agenda was the Saudi continuing investment in the Red Sea minerals extraction project estimated at about 4 billion dirhams or $1.08 billion dollars. In addition there was discussed the establishment of the Nadak wheat project, the largest Arab project for the cultivation of pulses (dried seeds) and fruits in the world at a cost of $13.1 billion dollars. These were among the Saudi commitments to be included in the Amman Declaration on large investment projects in the Middle East.

There were also projects announced by a number of GCC Emeriti, the Kingdom of Jordan and Lebanon.

- The United Arab Emirates committed to financing of one of the largest palm-growing projects in the Sudan, involving 225 million trees.

- The Kingdom of Jordan announced funding of a large self-sufficiency rice crop project in the Sudan.

- Kuwait committed to funding a 67,000 cattle project in the Sudan for export of beef to its market

- Lebanon announced funding for the largest feed project in the city of White Nile.

- A joint Bahrain and Qatar project was announced to grow fruits and legumes in Sennar near the Nile.

These projects encompass more than 12 million feddans or approximately 13 million agricultural acres in Sudan, one of the largest Arab integration projects in the world.

The Deepening Economic Ties between Sudan and the UAE

In February 2015, there were preliminary economic development discussions between Sudan President al-Bashir and Abu Dhabi Crown Prince Mohammed bin Zayed al-Nahyan and UAE Vice-President Mohammed bin Rashid al-Maktoum in Abu Dhabi. This culminated in March 2017 announcements in advance of the Amman Arab League summit. Those announcements were the latest manifestation of the economic benefits that have accrued to President al-Bashir for ending his long-term relationship with Tehran in 2014. A March 7, 2017, *Sudan Tribune* article reported:

> During his visit last month, al-Bashir discussed with the Crown Prince of Abu Dhabi Mohamed bin Zayed Al Nahyan ways to enhance economic and development cooperation. The Sudanese President pointed that directives were issued to the UAE ministers to work with Sudan in the various fields.

According to Sudan Minister Abdel-Ghani, the meeting discussed the current production projects especially the fattening and slaughterhouse schemes besides the vegetables and oilseeds projects. "We have developed an integrated vision in coordination with the industrial sector and now we are in the process of determining the sites and signing the contracts,"

Sudan President Bashir flanked by Crown Prince Mohammed bin Zayed al-Nahyan and UAE VP Mohammed bin Rashid Abu Dhabi 2-22-15

he said. The Sudanese minister pointed out that the delegation includes representatives of various UAE companies registered in Europe.

Sudan managed to achieve a breakthrough in ties with UAE after a long period of strained relations over Khartoum's close ties with Tehran.

The UAE is in a long-standing territorial dispute with Iran over the three Gulf islands of Abu Musa and Greater and Lesser Tunb.

Iran refuses international arbitration over the dispute and insists that its sovereignty over the islands is non-negotiable.

In 2014, Sudanese authorities ordered the closure of the Iranian cultural center in Khartoum, and other states in a move, which was seen as a gesture to the Arab Gulf states.

The estimated size of UAE investments in Sudan is approximately $11 billion of which about $5 billion are projects in progress while the rest are still in pre-execution phase. In May 2015, Sudan said it offered UAE's companies $59 billion dollars of investment opportunities mainly in agricultural projects.

Following the Arab League Summit at which tens of billions of dollars of infrastructure and agriculture projects were announced by Saudi Arabia and the Gulf Cooperation Council Emeriti, indicted war criminal President Bashir has been busy negotiating and inking these 'strategic deals'.

Sudan Tribune reported on April 11, 2017, "Sudan's Bashir, Kuwait's Sabah discusses bilateral relations:"

Al-Bashir and his accompanying delegation Tuesday arrived in Kuwait on a two-day official visit upon an invitation from the Kuwaiti Emir. The Emir and a number of senior officials received them at Kuwait airport.

The two sides held a round of talks on bilateral relations besides regional and international issues of common concern and they are expected to sign a number of agreements on joint cooperation in the various domains.

Also, the meetings discussed Kuwait's support for the Arab food security plan that was approved by the Arab leaders at their recent meeting in Amman.

During the meetings of the 3rd Arab Economic and Social Development Summit in Riyadh in 2013, al-Bashir launched an initiative to achieve Arab food security through offering investment opportunities in agriculture and livestock in Sudan.

Last February, Sudan's Investment Minister, Mudathir Abdel-Ghani said his country offered 220 investment projects to achieve the food security plan, pointing that Arab agricultural and livestock investment in Sudan represents 85% of the total foreign investment in the two sectors.

Bahrain's Visit

Meanwhile, Sudan's Foreign Minister Ibrahim Ghandour Monday said al-Bashir would fly to Bahrain after his visit to Kuwait at the invitation of Bahrain's King Hamad bin Isa Al-Khalifa.

Ghandour told reporters that al-Bashir and Al Khalifa will hold bilateral talks but he didn't give any further details.

It is noteworthy that al-Bashir is accompanied by the Minister of the Presidency, Fadl Abdallah Fadl; Foreign Minister, Ibrahim Ghandour; Finance Minister Badr al-Din Mahmoud and Minister of Water Resources, Electricity and Dams, Moataz Moussa.

Sudan's relations with the Gulf States have witnessed a thaw since late 2015 after years of tensions over Khartoum's close ties with Tehran.

This was followed by a *Sudan Tribune* article on April 12, 2017, "Gulf countries, Sudan to sign partnership agreement: Bashir;"

> Al-Bashir arrived in the Bahrain's capital Manama where he was welcomed by Bahrain's King Hamad bin Isa Al-Khalifa. He arrived from Kuwait where he held talks with the Emir Sheikh Sabah Al-Ahmad Al-Jaber Al-Sabah.
>
> Following a meeting with Al-Khalifa, al-Bashir confirmed to the official SUNA that the GCC countries would sign a strategic partnership agreement with Sudan. So, the Red Sea country will strengthen economic and trade ties with the Gulf countries.
>
> In a meeting with the Sudanese community in Kuwait on Tuesday, Foreign Minister Ibrahim Ghandour disclosed the partnership deal and said an agreement will be signed during a meeting of GCC foreign ministers to be held soon.
>
> The GCC countries have signed two similar agreements with the other monarchy regimes in Jordan and Morocco. The partnership includes financial aid, investments security and military cooperation.
>
> Sudan's active participation in the Saudi-led partnership military alliance waging war against the Iran-supported Shiite Houthi in Yemen and the massive agricultural investments in the Red Sea country prompted the partnership agreement.

In an interview with the Kuwait News Agency on Wednesday, Ghandour said: "Sudan has prepared a list of 220 development projects of which 79 ones were good to go." He further expressed hope that Kuwait would participate in providing support to these ventures.

Bashir discussed the Arab food security initiative, which calls to invest in Sudan agricultural projects with Al-Sabah and Al-Khalifa. The other GCC countries including Saudi Arabia, Qatar and the Arab United Emirates have already invested in these projects.

With the influx of billions of dollars in Saudi and GCC funds, Khartoum now has the financial underwriting for its 'final solution' for Darfur and South Kordofan giving it a free hand to exploit their gold deposits. Perhaps the long sought gold Arabia and, previously, $1.22 billion dollars from Qatar. Riyadh and Abu Dhabi production in these regions might back its faltering currency. Moreover, the profits from joint ventures with the Saudis would aid in launching its mercenary Jihad Army to create a Caliphate across most of the Sahel region of sub–Sahara Africa. It also may have the Saudi Kingdom's support to intercede on its behalf to end the 20-year international sanctions regime.

Conclusion

The objective of this strategic alliance with the Saudis and the Gulf Emeriti is to transform the Sudan into the virtual breadbasket for the Sunni Arab confederation in the Middle East. This economic integration plan would imply support for the strategic goal of the Khartoum regime's Arab Coalition Plan, as discussed on Chapter Five, "Revealed: Bashir's Secret Jihad Plan for Sudan."

Tens of billions of dollars of Saudi and Emeriti funded projects announced at the Arab League Summit and concluded in April 2017 provides economic incentives for fulfillment of Bashir's Jihad and Caliphate plans for the Sudan and ultimately the Sahel region. This upwelling of Sunni Arab support for the Sudan followed President al-Bashir's switch of alliance in 2014 from the Shiite Islamic Republic of Iran.

The trigger for this strategic investment program may have been signaled by the partial lifting of long-term US sanctions against the Bashir regime by the outgoing Obama Administration just prior to the inauguration of President Trump on January 20, 2017.

These billion dollar economic development integration projects in Sudan funded by Saudi Arabia and Emeriti members of the GCC may have played a part in former President Obama partially lifting the US sanctions against the Sudan. As we noted in Chapter Four, "President Bashir's 'Peace Force' perpetrates Jihad," the respite has not stopped Genocide in Darfur, the Nuba Mountains and the Blue Nile region. If anything the relentless Jihad against indigenous people in these Sudan regions has been more focused on their replacement with Arab tribes and foreign fighters. This may have been a factor behind statements made by US Rep. Jim McGovern, co-chairman of the bi-partisan US Congressional Human Rights Commission, calling for the introduction of new legislation in the 115th Congress re-instating Sudan sanctions. (See: "Chapter Three: Obama's Folly: Executive Order No. 13761 temporarily Lifting Sudan Sanctions".)

Chapter Eight
the price for lifting US Sudan Sanctions: Genocide

Janjaweed militias threatening life in Darfur

Sudan's volatile security situation and human rights abuses have worsened despite the partial lifting of sanctions by former President Obama, just days before the onset of the Trump Administration in January 2017. Under the terms of that partial sanctions lifting, there is a six months 'look back' period which could be reversed, if evidence of ethnic cleansing, genocide or support for Jihad terrorism persisted. This report graphically presents evidence that genocide, war crimes and human rights abuses have not ended in Darfur, Kordofan, and Blue Nile regions of the Sudan. Random killings, torturing, rape and extra-judicial executions continue unabated in all parts of these regions. There is evidence of aerial bombing attacks and the alleged use of banned chemical weapons. Syria is not the only Muslim country in the Middle East and Africa where indiscriminate use of weapons of mass destruction have been used against civilian populations. This has been delivered by bombing attacks of the Sudan Air force. Both China and Russia are supplying weapons and equipment in support of Sudan's genocidal Jihad funded by Gulf Emirates and Saudi Arabia. Time for the Trump Administration to re-impose Sudan sanctions and to consider establishing no-fly safe zones in Sudan conflict areas.

Over 119 people were killed in South Kordofan in early April 2017 and the fighting continues. This is another tragedy wrought by President Bashir with funding support from the Arab cabal of Qatar and Saudi Arabia. The massacre of 119 Harmar and Kababiish tribal people comes in the wake of a $200,000,000 gift from Her Royal Highness Sheikha Mozah Bint Naser of Qatar donated while on a recent trip to Sudan for the purpose of helping children in the Kordofan region. As we have written previously, the actual use of those funds was to support recruitment and arm more Janjaweed Arab "peace force" militias.

The Sudan Tribune reported Kababiish tribesmen shot and killed 36 people of the Hamar tribe. These people had their hands tied, were shot, slaughtered and their bodies burned and buried. According to Ambassador Hassan Ibrahim Jadkerim, those involved in the massacre were wearing Sudan regime's military uniforms and were armed with heavy weapons provided by the government.

According to the eye witness report, the fighting erupted between the two tribes of Hamar and Kababiish because of alleged stolen camels, despite both tribes using government supplied weapons and trucks killing each other. Both tribes are trained and armed by the government and they are part of the Janjaweed peace forces militias. The current governor of South Kordofan, Ahmed Harun, an indicted war criminal wanted for arrest by the International Criminal Court (ICC), has been organizing, training and arming these militias to attack the people of Darfur, Blue Nile and South Kordofan. He is directly responsible for these government-trained militias, financially sponsored by the State of Qatar. Fighting has been going on between these two tribes since the beginning of April 2017. Instead of providing security protection, the Sudan regime National Intelligence and Security Service (NISS) is supporting both conflicting groups with both weapons and logistic supplies.

The Sudan regime NISS security apparatus recruits, organizes, trains and arms these tribes with heavy weapons. The regime also provides them with trucks and logistic supplies. Moreover, the Bashir regime has granted them with full authority to kill anyone who opposes the implementation of the Arab Coalition plan directed at establishing a virtual Caliphate making demographic changes in Darfur and in the entire African Sahel region.

The Janjaweed peace forces Arab militias were established to enable the survival of the Bashir regime, fomenting international Jihad terrorism; the end state of the Muslim Brotherhood organization of the Islamic movement. The Bashir regime duplicitously arms these Arab militias. However, when they committed heinous crimes, such as the massacring innocent civilians, the regime will deny that it had connections with them calling them outlawed groups. It is the regime's strategy arming such groups and denying them when they committed crimes, so that they did not have to reveal that to the public and the international community. Effectively, the regime would eliminate any Arab militia group that refused to recruit its militants to fight for the regime. The fighting between Kababiish and Hamar is not the first instance of Arab militias fighting among themselves. It is an example of the internecine war to eliminate those opposing the Bashir regime to implement the strategy of the Arab Coalition (see Appendix B).

Arson and Killing in Darfur

The Sudan NISS and its armed Janjaweed peace force militias continue executing innocent civilians. They are massacring people, robbing, seizing of properties, committing arson and raping women. This is in furtherance of its strategy to dismantle Internally Displaced Persons (IDP) camps. The regime intelligence apparatus recruited and trained individuals unleashing them to conduct arson of homes in IDP camps and markets. Since late March 2017, several IDP camp homes and shops were burned in Nertiti, Zalengi, Central Darfur and Greida in South Darfur, and Garsila, in the Western Darfur region. These fires destroyed homes, food supplies, clothes and belongings of the IDP residents. Losses from this arson in Greida alone were estimated at approximately $3 million US dollars. The government's intention is to force the IDP camp residents into cities or move elsewhere so their land and wells are left to Arab Janjaweed peace force new settlers.

The National Congress Party Sudan regime is surviving only through crisis. The regime's security apparatus instigates such crises just to create confusion among Arab Janjaweed peace force militia and Darfur people, alike, and keep them busy fighting among themselves. The tribal clashes in Darfur and Kordofan regions are using government provided arms killing hundreds of people. These clashes are fomented, logistically supported and controlled by the NISS.

On March 31, 2017 nine Janjaweed militia fighters riding camels attacked a group of villagers driving their livestock to Tawal Shala water wells in eastern Jebel Marra. The militias opened fire and killed 3 people on the spot while others being pursued escaped for their lives. They seized all the possessions of those people killed including cows, donkeys and goats.

On April 3, 2017 Janjaweed militias shot and killed two brothers, Ali Ismael and Hamad Ismael. They were caught with their motorcycle in the Kasab IDP camp, Kutum, North Darfur.

On April 6, 2017 another group of Janjaweed militias riding camels intercepted a vehicle between Buram and Greida killed one man and wounded two others then robbed the passengers.

Human violations in Darfur have continued for more than fifteen years. In addition to Janjaweed militias' attacks, the Sudan government planes continue air bombardment on Jebel Marra and elsewhere. On April 6, 2017 Sudanese war-planes dropped bombs in the area west of Dereibat.

These attacks demonstrate that the Sudan regime and its militias target innocent civilians and their property.

Why Obama Lifted Sanctions on Sudan

Why did the former Obama Administration lift sanctions on Sudan if its militias continued to kill innocent people? Over 3 million people of Darfur are now living in IDP and refugee camps and Janjaweed militias occupy their land.

By lifting partial economic sanctions President Obama ignored long-standing US commitments to put an end to Sudan's years of internal conflicts and security instability caused by the National Islamic Front/Muslim Brotherhood regime. Former US President Obama's cooperation with the Islamic regime in Khartoum undermined United States engagement that might have prevented human right violations and protected indigenous populations targeted for ethnic cleansing by the Sudan regime. Instead, the Obama Administration's inaction in the face of these humanitarian violations by President Bashir was pursued in the vain hope of obtaining of counterterrorism intelligence information. Effectively, the Bashir regime provided little useful information and cooperation with US in the global war on terrorism. The National Islamic/Muslim Brotherhood regime continued to recruit, harbor and support terrorist organizations including fighters from the Islamic State. Obama's cooperation with the Sudan's indicted President Bashir compounded the problem by opening a door for other Western governments, such as Great Britain, Italy and Germany to establish various types of bilateral and multilateral economic and security cooperation agreements despite the Bashir regime's worsening human rights record.

Failure of African Union-United Nations Hybrid Operation in Darfur

The African Union-United Nations Hybrid Operation in Darfur (UNAMID) deployed in Darfur since 2007 with the mandate to protect civilians has unfortunately has become a puppet of the National Congress Party regime of President Bashir. Since its inception in Darfur, none of the UNAMID Secretaries have reported human right violations in Darfur. None of the UNAMID forces have protected any civilian that has his or her life threatened by the Janjaweed militias. Most of the killing, rape, torture, and other human right abuses committed by the Janjaweed occur close to or in the vicinity of UNAMID camps. The Janjaweed militias commit these crimes because they know the regime's security forces, which are mainly Janjaweed militias themselves, strictly control UNAMID's movement. That is the reason UNAMID forces could not investigate incidents or protect innocent civilians even one kilometer outside their camp.

The UNAMID forces cannot move without obtaining permission from the Sudan regime. Effectively, they cannot file a report or conduct an independent investigation without consulting the Sudan regime's officials and its security forces.

Failure of UNAMID to investigate incidents and write independent reports is probably the main reason that the international community distanced itself from Darfur. Darfurian people were internationally neglected and abandoned because UNAMID forces deployed to protect them had no capability to freely conduct operations.

Aicha El-Basri reveals UN cover up of Darfur Genocide

Aicha El-Basri, previously employed by UNAMID as spokesperson

Aicha El Basri, the former UNAMID spokesperson revealed confidential information that UN officials were unwilling to accept the fact that Sudan regime is deeply involved in mass killing of civilian population. She said,

> I believe in the UN, I wanted to serve the peacekeeping mission being transparent. But I did not receive any information. They even deliberately exclude me to inform the press about what I saw. Only *Radio Dabanga* reported the truth, not UN. I was astonished.
>
> First, I thought it was incompetence-for example, I had to find out from *Radio Dabanga* that UN peacekeepers were kidnapped-but I

found out that it was a policy, ordered by the mission's leadership to withhold information.

After they refused to tell the truth, I thought it was time to break the silence. I resigned from my UN position and decided to release all information the people need to know what is going on.

On her interview to *Asharq Al-Awsat*, she accused UNAMID Chief Mr. Mohammed Ibn Chambas, Mr. Herve Ladsous and UN Secretary General Ban Ki-Mon of complicity with the Sudanese regime of concealing the information of crimes the Arab militias committing on the population. It's clearly evident that UNAMID official's conspiracy to cover up the Sudan regime's crimes -committing against the people of Darfur.

Peace that includes all the people of Sudan will not come without support of US Congress and US Administration. Peace in Sudan will not come without replacement of Bashir and disarming the Janjaweed and all militia and removing terrorist groups from Sudan.

The Khartoum regime has no intentions of making peace in Sudan. The regime is using peace negotiations and dialogue as a means of deceiving the international community to allow it to remain in power and continue atrocities against the vulnerable population of. What has been achieved from these false peace negotiations and false peace agreements signed whether in Abuja, Nigeria, Doha, Qatar or elsewhere? Have any of these been initiatives that the victims of this genocide could sign that guarantee the end of the official Arab Coalition Plan?

The United Nations Security Council must appoint qualified officials who are impartial and empowered with the capacity to speak truthfully and act against the menace of genocide. Peace and justice for the Sudanese people must prevail.

The UNSC has no capability to force Sudan's regime to stop human right violations. Moreover, the Bashir regime has the power to dismiss any UN employee working in Sudan. The UNSC cannot protect them. Ivo Freijsen the Coordinator of Humanitarian Affairs in Sudan was expelled. Over the last two years the Bashir regime expelled four UN officials from Sudan while the UNSC did nothing. Sudan simply did not recognize any of the UNSC resolutions. The UNSC issued over 18 resolutions on Darfur, but none of these resolutions were implemented.

Indicted President Bashir has not been committing genocide alone without aid from Arab countries. China and Russia supply arms. Kuwait, Saudi Arabia, Qatar, European Union and some European states provide financial assistances that ends up recruiting and training Janjaweed Militias, Rapid Support Forces or what President Bashir calls 'peace forces.' African Union and many Arab League member states collectively provide protection for Bashir to avoid arrest and prosecution by the ICC.

Conclusion

The Chinese and Russians are providing weapons that Sudan President Bashir uses to kill our people. Arab countries and the European Union provide funds that are funneled to finance the recruitment of Janjaweed peace force militias that commit genocide against indigenous people of Sudan. We seek US and international assistance to stop the genocidal Jihad regime of President Bashir by seeking his arrest and establishing no-fly zones in Darfur, Kordofan and the Blue Nile region to save the lives of the country's indigenous people.

Chapter Nine
Sudan resistance commanders present the case to Congress on Retaining Sudan Sanctions

On April 26, 2017, the US House of Representatives Subcommittee on Africa, Global Health and Human Rights held a hearing on The Questionable Case for Easing Sanctions Sudan Sanctions The issue arose with the partial lifting by President Obama, just prior to leaving office in January 2017, of the 20-year economic sanctions against the Khartoum Regime of indicted war criminal Sudan President Omar Hassan al-Bashir. A provision of the partial lifting of Sudan sanctions was a six-month look back to determine if acts of terrorism and genocide have continued against the indigenous African people especially in Darfur, the Nuba Mountains, South Kordofan and the Blue Nile Region.

The hearings were chaired by Rep. Chris Smith (R-4th CD NJ) and Ranking Member Rep. Karen Bass (D -37th CD CA). Among the witnesses who are slated to appear are:

Mr. Brad Brooks-Rubin
Policy Director
The Sentry
[full text of statement]

·

Mr. David Dettoni
Senior Advisor
Sudan Relief Fund
[full text of statement]

·

Mr. Mohamed Abubakr
President
The African Middle Eastern Leadership Project
[full text of statement]

The Honorable Princeton N. Lyman
Senior Advisor to the President
United States Institute of Peace
[full text of statement]

Watch the archived video webcast of the hearing:

The preceding chapters attest to the continuing ethnic cleansing and genocide of indigenous peoples in these conflict regions, citing specific instances of Khartoum Regime backed Janjaweed Militia, now renamed Rapid Support Force (RSF) or Peace Forces, engaged in ethnic cleansing of villages and Internally Displaced Person Camps. The Janjaweed RSF Peace force is under the control of the National Intelligence Security Service (NISS) and Sudan Armed Force (SAF) Command. These reports have also revealed a Secret Arab Coalition Plan that would replace indigenous people with Arab tribes to be completed prior to 2020. In many instances, jihadist terrorists have been recruited from across the Sahel region and the Middle East. The objective of the Arab Coalition Plan is to resettle them in the lands formerly occupied by African tribal people with a view to creating a 150,000 man Jihad Army to create a Sharia-ruled Caliphate across the Sahel. The Arab Coalition Plan of the Khartoum Regime of President Bashir has the financial backing of the Emeriti members Gulf Cooperation Council and Saudi Arabia. These Jihadi recruits have been trained and organized in more than 16 camps in the Khartoum Region and equipped with arms and militarized pickup trucks. Further, there have been instances where the Janjaweed/ RSF Peace Forces have used prohibited chemical weapons of mass destruction coupled with bombings by Russian-supplied Antonov cargo planes of the Sudan Air Force on indigenous populations. And despite the evidence of abetting regional Islamic terrorism, the USAFRICOM, pursuant to so-called evidence of counterterrorism cooperation by the Bashir regime has included it in quarterly security reviews at its headquarters in Stuttgart, Germany.

For these reasons, the authors solicited witness testimony from Sudan resistance leaders in Darfur and the Nuba Mountains exposing the Bashir regime's Jihad genocide objectives of the Arab Coalition Plan.

Testimony of Lt. Gen. Abakar M. Abdallah
Chairman of the Sudan United Movement (SUM)
Submitted to the US House of Representatives
Subcommittee on Africa and Global Human Rights

I wish to apprise the Subcommittee of the status of the Jihad genocide being committed in Darfur by the National Congress Party (NCP) regime of indicted war criminal, Sudan President Omar al-Bashir. The facts on the ground in Darfur do not justify continuing the partial lifting of US Sanctions against the Bashir Regime. Moreover, the regime is pursuing aggressive ethnic cleansing of Darfurian indigenous African people and their replacement with Arab tribes and international terrorist groups recruited for the NCP Regime Rapid Support Forces (RSF-Reorganized Janjaweed militias).

President Bashir's Rapid Support Forces (RSF) continually pillages and loots everything from the villages and the Internally Displaced Population Camps in Darfur. They rape women, burn homes, destroy water sources, damage crops, seize grazing animals on farms and fruit plantations. President Bashir's objective is to inflict poverty and entirely remove the population of Darfur from their land and replace them with new settlers the regime brings in from foreign states. Bashir's NCP regime continually commits Genocide on the people of Darfur, Kordofan, and the Blue Nile. Therefore, there is an urgent need to stop him from committing further atrocities.

The current security situation is worse and human right abuses in Darfur are continuing despite the fact that President Obama partially lifting Sudan's twenty years of US economic sanctions imposed at the result of President Bashir's support of terrorism and violation of human rights. The actions of genocide, war crimes and human right abuses have not ended in Darfur, Kordofan, and Blue Nile that have occurred for over 15 years. The situation remains the same.

Killing, torturing, rape and ejection continue in all parts of Darfur, Kordofan and the Blue Nile. Furthermore, the regime continues recruiting, training, and financing of Arab tribal militias and terrorism. Former US President Obama's cooperation with the Islamic regime in Khartoum undermined United States engagement directed at preventing human right violations and protection of the innocent population targeted by the Sudan regime's long years of brutality.

We request the US Subcommittee on Africa to urge President Trump's Administration to reverse President Obama's decision and reinstate vigorous economic sanctions against the Sudan regime. Further, we are requesting assistance for the Sudan United Movement to disarm Janjaweed militias leading to possible regime change in Sudan. This would assist in establishing a democratic system of government that respects the rights of all Sudanese people.

While Obama partially lifted economic sanctions against the genocidal Bashir regime, its Janjaweed militias, renamed "Peace Forces", massacred over 80 people in Nertiti and Geneina in Central and Western Darfur regions in early January 2017. The indicted war criminal President Omar Hassan Ahmed al-Bashir's Islamic Peace Forces have been committing genocide, war crimes and crimes against the African population of non-Arab origin since the 1980s. Following the partial lifting of economic sanctions, the Regime's "Desert Shield" Militias killed and wounded over 119 people in Sodari, South Kordofan in April 2017. The massacring of over 119 innocent civilians by the Bashir's militias illustrates the regime's continual human rights violation not only in Darfur but also in the other conflict regions of Sudan. Nothing has changed on the ground.

With the objective of furthering the Islamic extremist ideology, they have extended killing to the innocent population of the adjacent Central African Republic and Chad. This is all part of the National Congress Party regime's plan to establish through ethnic cleansing of African tribes a Caliphate in the Sahel sub-region of Northern Africa.

The regime recruits, trains, organizes these militias and provides them with trucks, arms and logistic supplies. It unleashes them with full authority to kill anyone who opposes the implementation of the Arab Coalition policies, which seek to make demographic changes not only in Darfur but also in the whole African Sahel Sub-region culminating in the establishment of a Caliphate. The primary role of the Arab militias is to ensure the survival of the regime and create a veritable Jihadist army under the banner of the Islamic movement of the Muslim Brotherhood.

On April 18, 2017, the regime deployed 7,000 militia, some of whom were brought in from Libya and had been organizing and training in the area of Jelly, Kabcabiyia, and North Darfur. They were organizing and deploying these militias in line with the regime's policies to implement the Arab Coalition Plan (see

Appendix B). The Arab Coalition Plan was found in the Arabic Language version of 11 pages captured during the fighting between the Rapid Support Forces (RSF) (Reorganized Janjaweed Militias) and Darfur rebels in October of the year 2014 in Donkey Hush, North Darfur. The document was found in an abandoned military truck of the RSF.

The document contains statements or evaluations of the Arab Coalition project that began in 1987 and has been continuously updated through the last evaluation in 2014. The objective of President Bashir's regime and its Janjaweed militias is to eradicate the people of Darfur and occupy the land. We have translated the document into English to reveal what is behind the Arab coalition organization in cooperation with the Khartoum regime creating and arming of Janjaweed militias.

The most important part of the document is the evaluation of 2014 in which they distribute the entire Darfur region to different Arab tribes. They intend to finish their project prior to the year 2020. If the Arab Coalition Plan is left unchecked and Janjaweed militias are not disarmed, the genocide human rights atrocities in Darfur will continue. The Arab Coalition is not only supported by the Bashir regime but also by the Arab League and Arab governments in Middle East.

It is unfortunate that Darfur people become prey to the oil rich Middle East Arab States, who stand firmly behind Bashir supporting him financially and politically. The worse thing is to see the international community embracing the Arab regime of Khartoum and witness African countries not only distancing themselves from Darfur but not even understanding what is the real cause of the problem. They just blindly support Bashir's genocidal regime. Darfur genocide is one of the world's longest genocides and is visible to all. Darfur's problem is more than the conflict between the Darfur resistance movements and the Bashir regime. It is the Arab policy of establishing a Caliphate in the African Sahel region. We request the US government address this crisis not as simply conflict between two parties. This conflict has three parties: (1) indigenous people or original citizens of Darfur, (2) the new Arab settlers that the regime brings from foreign countries that constitutes the Janjaweed militias; and, (3) the Khartoum regime and its Arab Cabal, notably Saudi Arabia and State of Qatar, that supports President Bashir financially.

Why did President Bashir select Darfur to be used as baseline to create a Caliphate in the African Sahel Region? Geographically Darfur occupies a strategic location linking the African sub-Sahara Sahel region Middle East and Europe through the vast Sahara desert to the Mediterranean Sea and the Atlantic Ocean. The region is an important strategic location in the continent linking West African nations and North Africa. Since the early days of Islam, the Darfur region has been a crossing point where people coming from different directions met.

Based on its strategic location, the Sudan government makes this region a hub for all extremist and transnational terrorist groups.

These groups include al Qaeda, Janjaweed, and Lord's Resistance Army (LRA) currently present in areas of Merlin Camp and Ain al Khadra near Kafia Kingi and Mountain Abu-Rassin Central African Republic (CAR), Mali Jihadists, Boko Haram, and ISIS. These groups are integrated in the RSF, while Central African rebels are currently operating with some SELEKA factions in CAR. Others include South Sudan rebels, Chadian rebels, and ISIS. These groups are trained and organized in Sudan prior to sending to their various regions of operation. One example is the South Sudan Islamic Liberation Movement that Ali Tamim Fartak has organized in Niyala, capital the South Darfur region. These groups regularly move back and forth between the countries in the region, the Middle East, North Africa, and Europe. Darfur is a land locked region that links all the roads from sub-Saharan Africa going to Middle East, Egypt and Europe via the Red Sea and the Mediterranean Sea.

The Forces of the African Union-United Nations Hybrid Operation in Darfur (UNAMID) were initially deployed in 2007 in Darfur with the mandate to protect civilians. Unfortunately, these forces came under the strict control of the Sudan's regime. Therefore, it could not conduct independent operations without permission from the Sudan's security forces. As a result, it has become completely ineffective and consequently failed to provide security for the vulnerable indigenous Darfurian population. Neither could it write credible reports on human right violations carry out by the Janjaweed militias. The organization became in effect a puppet of the National Congress Party regime of President Bashir.

Since the inception of UNAMID in Darfur none of its reports on human right violations and none of its forces protect any civilians threatened by the Janjaweed militias. Most of the killing, rape, torture, and other human right abuses in Darfur pass without recording and notification of the international community because of the ineffectiveness of UNAMID force deployed in Darfur. For example, when UNAMID reported that regime security forces conducted mass rape of 200 women in Tabit; the Sudan regime summoned its chief representative and threatened to withdraw its forces from Sudan. Since then none of the UN or AU agents have spoken of the Tabit mass rape that occurred in 2015.

Brought peace in Darfur? Why do we believe that this regime wants to bring peace?

The US bilateral talks were held at the time, while the NCP government in Khartoum continuously finances and provides safe havens to international terrorists and their organizations. The Islamic extremist regime of Khartoum used negotiations with Obama's Administration to attack the civilian population in Jebel Marra using weapons of mass destruction. The Amnesty International's report "Scorched Earth Poisoned Air" report issued on September 29, 2016 presented a credible explanation of the use of smoke type chemical agents. The organization interviewed several people from Jebel Marra and provided pictures of the victims exposed to these prohibited chemical agents. As a result, we recommend to US Congress urge President Trump's Administration not to help NCP regime escape responsibility for crimes it is committing against the people of Sudan.

Under the cover of these false peace deals Russian supplied Antonov cargo planes continually drop bombs on population settlements including chemicals agents. Janjaweed militias continue massacring and plundering unprotected populations and properties in Darfur. Women are systematically raped at gunpoint. Following these 'peace deals' for Darfur, more people are displaced, more villages are burned, more men are tortured and killed, more women are raped, and more atrocities are committed.

This is not the first time the NCP regime has been accused of using weapons of mass destruction in Sudan. It used them in South Sudan in 1999 and again in South Kordofan and Blue Nile in 2016. Despite several reports accusing the radical Islamic government of using prohibited weapons, the United Nation Security Council (UNSC) has done nothing. It is unfair and unacceptable for UNSC to maintain silence and not question President Bashir or investigate the episodes in Jebel Marra on the use of chemical weapons. We request US government investigate the Bashir regime's use of chemicals weapons and treatment of wounded victims.

In Conclusion

President Bashir of Sudan continually commits genocide, war crimes, and crimes against humanity on the African population of non-Arab origin in Darfur, Kordofan, Blue Nile, and Darfur. President Bashir's failure to sign genuine peace agreements and breaching cease fires aggravated the security situation in conflict areas in Sudan that endangers the lives of the indigenous civilian population. President Bashir continually recruits trains, and arms Janjaweed militias and transnational terrorist groups causing the security instability of Sudan, notably in Darfur and the conflict areas. The true intention of President Bashir and his Janjaweed militias is to implement the Arab Coalition Plan we recovered from an abandoned Rapid Support Force truck in Donkey Hush, Darfur in 2014. What is happening in Darfur is continuous destruction of indigenous African population with intention to make a complete a total ethnic cleaning and demographic change?

Testimony of General Abdalaziz Adam Alhilu
SPLA/N General commander/Chief of staff of SPLA/N and
Deputy Chairman of the SPLM-N
Submitted to US House of Representatives
Subcommittee on Africa, Global Health and Global Human Rights
April 26, 2017

My name is General Abdalaziz Adam Alhilu, General Commander of the Sudan People's Liberation Army-North (SPLA-N in the Nuba Mountains). I thank you for the opportunity to present my views for consideration of the Subcommittee on African Affairs on the reinstatement of sanctions against the regime of Sudan President Omar al-Bashir. The hearing subject raises fundamental questions. What should be done to deter Khartoum from their murderous plan since sanctions do not work, what might really work? Also what we can do to make the new Administration in Washington, DC administration understand our problem?

The Nuba, Funj and Darfur were the first targets of the National Islamic Front (NIF) state sponsored terrorism against its own citizens for the last 30 years. That same behavior forced South Sudan to opt for independence. The NIF is using Sharia Islamic laws to rally the Arabs in the North and legitimize the ethnic cleansing and genocide against the Africans and Christians in Sudan.

Note that Islamic Jihad was declared against the Nuba people regardless of religion or belief in 1992, and it is still in effect as of today. The Arabs in the North are using the Jihad declaration by Muslim Clerics and the NIF to absolve themselves from any guilty conscience, when they raid, kill (3,000,000), burn villages (400,000), and rape, enslave loot and displace the African citizens and communities. In the name of Jihad, the Arabs organized themselves as PDF, Mujahideen, and Rapid Support Force (RSF) etc., to support the NIF (National

Islamic Front) Islamic Army or so called Sudan Armed Force (SAF) in that 'holy war' (Jihad).

That is the internal effect of the Sharia Laws. Externally, it is even far-reaching and dangerous to International peace and stability.

Since 1989 the NIF regime in Sudan turned into a strong hold for the Sunni International Islamic Movement (Muslim Brotherhood) worldwide. Sudan engaged in creating indoctrination and training ground for all Sunni based terrorist organizations (Al-Qaeda, ISIS, al-Nusra Front, and Boko Haram). Most people overlook Sudan, thinking Turkey is more dangerous. However, the Islamists in Turkey may be soon in full control of the state machinery to use it in the interest of the International Islamic Movement given the recent national referendum vote.

Others think Iran is more dangerous. While Iran may be leading Shiite sect, they are a minority in the Islamic world compared to Sunni Sects.

The International Islamic Movement represents the spearhead of the Pan Arabism Movement, pitted against the West in what has been called the Clash of Civilizations. Given the superiority of the West in terms of weaponry, the Islamists use strong nationalist zeal and hate to spearhead non-conventional warfare tactics and weapons to tilt the balance. 9/11 was an example. Something unexpected in the West, that Islamists would resort to using civil-aviation planes to execute the most dangerous terrorist operation in history targeting the iconic World Trade Center in New York, the Pentagon in northern Virginia and the White House in Washington, DC.

Let us remind ourselves that, the first attempt on the World Trade Centre in 1993 was organized and conducted by the Muslim Brotherhood. The bombings of the Nairobi and Dar es Salaam US Embassies in 1998 were perpetrated by bin Laden's Al Qaeda, an outgrowth of the Muslim Brotherhood.

In short, Sharia Laws and the terrorist nature of the Sudan regime are behind many of the internal and external problems we see today from the Sudan.

What should be done?

In order to end the genocide in Sudan, the USA should put more pressure on the Khartoum National Congress Party (NCP) regime of indicted war criminal President Omar al-Bashir to repeal and abrogate the Sharia Laws, in order to pave the way for peaceful and democratic transformation in the Sudan. This can be done through internationally supervised peace talks. If there is genuine secular and conventional democracy, the Islamists will not survive. They will transform over time, provided that they are deprived of the Sharia divine right to rule and terrorize using the resources of Sudan.

Removal of Sharia Laws, will stop Sudanese Islamists from enjoying state cover to practice terrorism and supporting Jihadists and terrorists globally from the Muslim *ummah*. It will stop human trafficking, money laundering and migration from Africa to the West. Khartoum is masterminding the destabilization in the Sub- Saharan Sahel Region and beyond in Chad, Central African Republic, Niger, Nigeria, Mali, Egypt and Libya.

Do not let the Bashir NCP regime in Khartoum fool anyone, with its deception plan. They say they can cooperate with the US and its allies in the war against terrorism. If they are not party to that, how could they get information about the terrorists? It is open political gaming with the Western intelligence agencies in order to have the sanctions against the NCP regime lifted. After lifting the sanctions they will resume and continue their old ways of support for Jihad and ethnic cleansing of indigenous African people in the Sudan and the Sahel.

They do not share common values of human rights, freedoms, rule of law with the USA, in order for them to provide all the information requested on the terrorist movements. They only trust their mentors and supporters of the International Islamic Movement.

Islamists can change on their own and deliver democratic transformation in Sudan and other countries. That is mere propaganda. The very nature of the organization and the Islamic teachings will prevent them from refraining from Jihad terrorism.

For the interest of peace and stability in Sudan, the Sahel region and internationally, the Bashir NIF / NCP regime should be have to be dismantled either peacefully or by force.

Thank you for the opportunity to present my views as Commander of the SPLA-North in the Nuba Mountains.

Testimony of Mr. Sodi Ibrahim,
Executive Director of the Sudan Relief and Rehabilitation Agency (SRRA-N)
Submitted to the US House of Representatives Subcommittee on Africa, Global Health and Global Human Rights
April 6, 2017

My name is Mr. Sodi Ibrahim. I am director of the Sudan Relief and Rehabilitation Agency (SRRA-N). I thank you for the opportunity to present my views for the consideration of the Subcommittee on Africa, Global Health and Global Human Rights on the reinstatement of US economic sanctions against the regime of Sudan President Omar al-Bashir. I will address what is behind the current Genocide in Sudan, why the Regime has policies of marginalizing indigenous African people, why Arabization of the conflict areas in Sudan have intensified, what is the status as of today and the resistance movement needs.

Genocide in the Sudan

The problem of Genocide in Sudan is a policy based on an Islamic belief system. Starting in 1881, Sharia Law was declared in Sudan by the Mahdi. He did this in direct defiance of an Ottoman Empire edict that exempted Sudan from implementation of Sharia. The Mahdi wanted a country that was fully Islamic for Arab peoples. The plan was made to slowly cleanse the land of the Black Skinned peoples (Abiid), as he believed was called for in the Koran.

This ethnic cleansing went on slowly by choosing to disadvantage and marginalize all black skinned people of any tribe. In the 1950's, a coalition to rule Sudan was formed by Sadiq al Mahdi, the al Mirghani family and Dr. Hassan al Turabi. The goal of this coalition was to Arabize the whole of Sudan, while looking to conquer all of Africa for the Islamic cause.

In 1964 Sadiq al Mahdi, descendent of the earlier Mahdi and one-time president of Sudan, gave a speech in the Cultural Center in Juba, Sudan in which he stated, "All you people (residents of Juba) need to leave Sudan. South Sudan is the stepping-stone to the Islamization of all of Africa. We do not want you here." The Government had adopted a policy of slow genocide.

The policies of marginalization continue.

In the 1980's, Al Qaeda brought Bin Laden and the Muslim Brotherhood with their fundamentalism to Sudan, which strengthened the desire for a fully Arab state. Sharia was declared again in 1983 by President Numeri. Dr. Hassan al Turabi and Sadiq al Mahdi during the same period preached that the Mahdi to come was arriving soon since 'it was the 14th century since the *hijrah* (migration from Mecca and Medina by the Prophet Mohammed), and the Mahdi is coming to take over the world and we must be ready with a fully Islamic country.'

There was a major Arab (Muslim Brotherhood) conference in 1985 led by Dr. Turabi. Turabi immediately began to work against Christians. The goal was to gradually eliminate them to cleanse the country. When Bashir came to power in 1989, his goal was to speed up the cleansing of the country. He brought a severe government to power, which used force to cause the Abiid and Kufr (infidels) to accept the Muslim Brotherhood form of Islam or be killed.

Arabization intensified

In 1994, Osama bin Laden from inside Sudan (with Bashir's agreement) declared a Holy War against the United States. Bin Laden was living in Sudan waging this holy war or Jihad. He had lived in Sudan from 1983 when Sharia was declared. Bashir supported Bin Laden with all the resources of Sudan. The Bin Laden Fatwa was a declaration of war on the US that has never been rescinded.

There was also a war declared by the Bashir regime on the non-Islamic and black-skinned people, as far as Khartoum was concerned. So the Khartoum Arab Government began destroying churches, burning people in them. The Arabs were using advanced weapons to destroy people. They used starvation, spread disease, withheld vaccinations, provided no education, and outlawed local languages and cultures. They attacked villages, raped women, and killed elders. They used any means to destroy the people of black skin, to cleanse the land.

They trained militias: Janjaweed, Miseriya, al Qaeda, Boko Haram, Joseph Kony's Lord Resistance Army, Somali, Malians, Libyans, Syrians, and international jihadi from all over the world. They built training camps and provided weapons. This was part of a two pronged strategy to: 1) take over and ethnically cleanse Sudan, and 2) ultimately take over and unify the world for Islam.

In November 1994 the Khartoum regime announced that they would never accept a government with separation of church and state making it clear that the "Arab only" form of Islam was in Sudan to stay and conquer the rest of Africa and the world.

Status as of today

The war declared against the US and the West has intensified yet again. Mujahideen trained in Sudan fight in Syria. They accept the ISIS warriors as heroes and resettle their families in the Sudan by giving them the land of Darfurians that the Janjaweed/Defense Shield have forced to flee from their homes. Recently, during SPLA-N fighting to stop these attacks the SPLA-N captured three Boko Haram International mujahideen sent to the Nuba Mountains to fight for Khartoum. These fighters reported that they were instructed to kill everyone.

In the last year, Khartoum has broken cease fires more than 12 times. Even following the US partially lifting the Sudan economic sanctions, the cease fire was broken within a few days. Now, Khartoum has used invested money against the black skinned Muslims and Christians to cleanse the land.

There have been 15 rounds of official negotiations to no avail.

Khartoum does not recognize the problem is its orders to kill the Abiid and others. No Sudanese can sign something that agrees to law that includes "kill the Abiid, Kufr, Christians, and Jews." The Sudanese have black skin why would anyone agree to commit genocide on yourself? Khartoum refuses anything but Sharia law, which calls for death of a majority of its citizens.

What do we need?

We need you to work with us. They are committing Genocide.

Right now they are killing us. We fight to defend ourselves, while they attack to kill and fulfill the obligations of the Koran.

Recently, 143 families ran to the bush to find roots, as there is no other food. They were attacked and now eight women are missing.

The UN has failed to stop this genocide, the sanctions have failed after 20 years of application

Genocide is supposed to be stopped by 'any means' according to international law - please help us!

Testimony of Yunan Musa Kunda, SSRA-N
External Relationship Coordinator
Submitted to the US House of Representatives, Subcommittee on Africa, Global Health and Global Human Rights
April 26, 2017

My name is Yunan Musa Kunda, Sudan Relief and Rehabilitation Agency North (SRRA-N) External Relationship Coordinator. I thank you for the opportunity to present my views for consideration of the Subcommittee on African Affairs on the reinstatement of sanctions against the regime of Sudan President Omar al-Bashir.

History of Genocidal War in Sudan

The war with Khartoum is a resistance war against the genocidal policies of this Arab Government that took over Sudan from the British in 1956. The Arab Government instituted Sharia Law, which they said calls for the extermination of the black population in the country. This Arab Government officially began reducing the black population by any means. People with black skin from many tribes all over Sudan resisted that effort. The Genocidal efforts of the Arab Government have not slowed genocide by many means since independence in 1956, even though many Arab leaders have come and gone.

From independence from the British to the Ananya Peace Agreement only one regime was considered to have committed genocide. Then from 1983, the resistance flared again, as the genocide from the Arabs intensified. Southern Sudan continued to resist the genocidal activities of Khartoum until independence in 2011.

What was the purpose of this genocide? It was to subjugate and remove black people in Sudan. The Government in Khartoum as late as 2016 stated that their goal was to kill all black-skinned people in the country or enslave them as they do in Mauritania. They do not want to see black- skinned people in the country of Sudan.

One of our heroes was Philip Gabush Yusef from the Nuba Mountains, who wanted peace. The Khartoum Arab Government put him in prison to stifle his voice.

The late Dr. John Garang fought because the Arab Khartoum Government berated black people. The South resisted Arabization until independence in 2011.

Another strategy of the Arab Khartoum government is to resist Christians. So "no Christians" is a slogan the Arab Government lives by. Right now in Khartoum another wave of bulldozing church buildings is going on. They are also burning churches and even health centers, which serve the black or Christian population.

The strategy of Arabization

Immigration is encouraged by the Arab government in Khartoum. In the last few months 3,000 Syrians have immigrated to Sudan and been given nationality papers and land that belonged to the black Sudanese the government displaced. Khartoum wants to change the demography of the country to be majority Arab. The immigration documents of those captured by the SPLA-N indicate Sudan as their country of origin when their language is not Sudanese of any sort. The reason for this strategy is to have the resources of the country in the hands of loyal Arabs rather than black citizens. So when the Janjaweed or Peace Forces displace citizens they want them to go to refugee camps or be killed to dispossess them of their land. If the refugees flee to South Sudan there is little food in the camps, few schools, and very few medical services. The UN does not supply enough food. The push by Khartoum is ejecting indigenous people from their land to not return.

Use of Weapons of Mass Destruction – Chemical agents

The most recent strategy that the Arab Government of Khartoum has deployed against the black population is Chemical Weapons of Mass Destruction, acquired from the late Saddam Hussein in 2002. This strategy was used in late 2016 just before the US lifted sanctions.

Conclusions

Lifting sanctions has only encouraged the Khartoum Arab regime to continue to kill the black population of the country whether Christian, Muslim or traditional religion. We are defending ourselves, yet, we are not the instigators of the violence here. We ask you to do more than reinstate the sanctions. We urge you to do whatever it takes to stop the genocide against black people in Sudan.

Chapter Ten
Chad and Libya cut Ties to Qatar and Sudan over terrorism support

President Idriss Deby of Chad

Contretemps arose in early June 2017 over Saudi Arabia, Emirates UAE, Bahrain, Egypt and Qatar's alleged support for the Muslim Brotherhood and terrorism. That led to exposure of Qatar, Sudan, Iran and Turkish support for the overthrow of Chad and the Libyan National Army regime of Marshal Khalifa Hafter.

On June 9, 2017, the government of Chad issued the following statement cutting diplomatic relations with Qatar. Chadian President Idriss Deby has long been waiting for this moment. Qatar has hosted and supported Chadian Islamist groups who have been recruited to overthrow his democratically elected government. The Chadian Islamists are also recruited as part of the Rapid Support Force (RSF)/Janjaweed miltias to fight proxy wars for indicted war criminal Sudan President Omar al-Bashir. Chad joins Egypt and other African nations condemning Qatar for support of Islamist terror groups like Hs in Gaza, Al Nusrah, the Al Qaeda affiliate in Syria, and the Muslim Brotherhood.

95

Qatar recently provided the Sudan with upwards of $200 million. These funds were ostensibly used to provide education for orphans in the Kordofan region. In reality, the funds were used for other purposes: (1) to support RSF/Janjaweed militia training camps in the Khartoum and Darfur regions; and, (2) to construct 1,200 villages in North Darfur for the settlement of arriving Janjaweed families. More than 24,000 RSF/Janjaweed militia forces graduated from the Bashir regime training camps in mid-May 2017 and some of those were immediately deployed to the Darfur region, Nuba Mountains and Blue Nile while some were deployed to jihad outside Sudan.

The RSF/Janjaweed are the basis for an estimated 150,000 Jihadist army that Bashir is recruiting from across the Sahel region of sub Sahara Africa and Middle East terrorist groups to ethnically cleanse indigenous African people in Sudan's Darfur, Nuba Mountains and Blue Nile conflict zones.

More than 5 million indigenous black African people had been internally displaced to IDP camps in Darfur. More than 600,000 have been killed in Darfur, along with in excess of 2 million killed in the six-decade internal jihad operations in the Sudan.

President Bashir's ultimate objective is to replace these indigenous black African people with Arab settlers from the RSF/Janjaweed forces and international mujahedeen to invade adjacent countries in a planned jihad across the Sahel region imposing a Caliphate ruled from Khartoum under Sharia Islamic law.

Presently, Bashir is joining with Kuwait seeking to assist in resolving the current impasse with Qatar over its support for Islamist terrorism.

Chad News issued this report:

> Chad cuts diplomatic ties with Qatar
>
> The Chadian government announced that it had cut off all diplomatic relations with Qatar and accused Doha of sponsoring terrorism in Africa. A statement issued by the Ministry of Foreign Affairs and Cooperation: "The Republic of Chad has on all occasions affirmed its strong commitment to defend Africa's supreme interests and its firm adherence to the principle of respect for the sovereignty of States, non-interference in their affairs and their continued efforts to consolidate security and stability in the continent of Africa and the world." Their positions have always reflected their firm belief in the need to strengthen cooperation and solidarity among brothers and to confront any threat to security and stability in Africa." Unfortunately, the State of Qatar has been working to undermine these principles on which the common African action is based. Its policy in the region has been linked to the support of terrorist organizations, the

promotion of extremist ideas and the spread of chaos and instability in many African countries, resulting in great human tragedies in those countries and in Europe and across the world. It also led to the dismantling of the institutions of sister States and the destruction of their infrastructure." Chad cut ties with Doha after Saudi Arabia, the United Arab Emirates, Bahrain, Egypt, Yemen, Mauritania, the Maldives and Mauritius, Republic of Senegal and Republic of Gabon.

Here was the Chadian press statement, translated from the original Arabic:

The Chadian government calls on all concerned countries to prefer dialogue as a means to resolve this crisis and calls on Qatar to respect its commitments to stop any action that could harm the cohesion of the countries in the region and peace in the world, "a foreign ministry statement said. The announcement came a day after Senegal recalled its envoy. Gabon condemned Qatar for failing to comply with international agreements on counter-terrorism. Mauritania and the Comoros also decided to cut off diplomatic ties with Qatar on Tuesday, June 6th. These African nations join a group of countries on Monday, June 5th cutting off relations with Qatar including Saudi Arabia, the United Arab Emirates, Bahrain, Egypt, Yemen, Libya, the Maldives and Mauritius.

Libyan National Army Marshall Khalifa Hafter
Libyan National Army revealed the Triad of Terror: Qatar, Sudan, Iran and Turkey

On June 22, 2017, Col. Ahmed Mismari, spokesman for the Libyan National Army (LNA) released a statement saying they had documentary evidence of collusion by Qatar, Sudan and Iran seeking to overthrow the regime of Marshal Khalifa Hafter. *The Libyan Herald* report noted:

> We have records of secret meetings of the Sudanese army leadership in the presence of [President Omar] Bashir [which show] a clear conspiracy with Qatar and Iran to support terrorism in Libya, Egypt [and] Saudi Arabia," he reported on the LNA's *Facebook* page
>
> At a press conference last night in Benghazi, he gave details of the alleged Sudanese collaboration with Qatar and Iran, stating that the latter two had military factories in Sudan, which were supplying weapons and ammunition to terrorists both in Libya and elsewhere.
>
> Like Qatar, he claimed, Sudan was actively supporting the Muslim Brotherhood in Libya and Egypt. The two were also actively working alongside Turkey and Iran.
>
> Evidence of Libyans working with Qatari intelligence had come from Qatar's opposition leader Khalid Al-Hail, Mismari claimed.
>
> Notwithstanding, reports of Sudanese mercenaries fighting both for and against the LNA, relations between the eastern authorities and Khartoum have progressively worsened in recent weeks, in no small part to the presence of of Sudanese among militants fighting the LNA in Benghazi. Some 20 are reported to have died fighting in Libya. Tuesday's suicide bomber in Sidra was also apparently a Sudani.

Jonathan Schanzer, Senior Vice President of the Washington, DC Foundation or Defense of Democracies in an August 6, 2017 *Newsweek* report, "Qatar's Support of The Worst of the Worst In Libya Must End" documented the long history of Qatar's support for extremist Islamist groups in Libya. He noted the following:

> Since the 2011 revolution, Libya has been the site of a rather nasty proxy war. The UAE, Saudi Arabia, Egypt, and other traditional Gulf states have backed the eastern-based government and Khalifa Haftar's Libyan National Army (LNA). Seeking a more Islamist order in Libya, Qatar and Turkey backed the Muslim Brotherhood, and more recently, the Tripoli-based General National Congress (GNC).
>
> According to press reports, Qatar has been sending massive amounts of weapons and cash to Islamist militants battling the Western-backed government in Libya. A March 2013 U.N. report noted that in 2011 and 2012, Qatar violated the U.N. arms embargo by "providing military material to the revolutionary

forces through the organization of a large number of flights and the deliveries of a range of arms and ammunition."

And according to another report in the Egyptian al-Masry al-Youm, Doha has provided more than 750 million euros ($890 million) to extremist groups in Libya since 2011. Arab officials believe that this assistance arrives in Western Libya by way of a commercial airline that is bankrolled by Qatar.

But the Arab states are not simply bothered by Qatar's support for garden variety Islamists. They allege that Qatar is directly backing the worst of the worst. And they appear to be correct.

According to Kristian Coates Ulrichsen of the Baker Institute for Public Policy, "Qatar developed close links with key Islamist militia commanders [in Libya] such as Abdelhakim Belhadj, once the head of the Libyan Islamic Fighting Group and, in 2011, the commander of the Tripoli Brigade." The LIFG is an al-Qaeda affiliate group that was sanctioned by both the United States and the United Nations.

Belhadj twice met with Osama bin Laden and was detained by the CIA in 2004. He launched Hizb al-Watan in 2012, which Arab officials say has maintained close ties to LIFG and received continued support from Qatar.

Ulrichsen also notes the connection between Qatar and "Ismael al-Salabi, the leader of one of the best-supplied rebel militias, the Rafallah al-Sahati Companies. Qatar was widely suspected of arming and funding al-Salabi's group, whose sudden munificence of resources in 2011 earned it the nickname of the 'Ferrari 17 Brigade.'"

Ismael al-Salabi's brother, Ali al-Salabi, is a prominent Libyan cleric close to the emir of Qatar. One Egyptian source claims that he maintains close ties to the LIFG. This is a claim echoed by Arab officials familiar with the situation in Libya.

The allegations of Qatari malign behavior in Libya continue. The Libyan army spokesman just last week described Qatar, Sudan, and Turkey as "the triad of terrorism" in Libya. He also stated that, "a number of Qatari aircraft are regularly landing in Libya in 2017 to support terrorist groups."

Then there is the peculiar Game of Thrones in Chad involving members of President Deby's family active in the Muslim Brotherhood supported by Qatar.

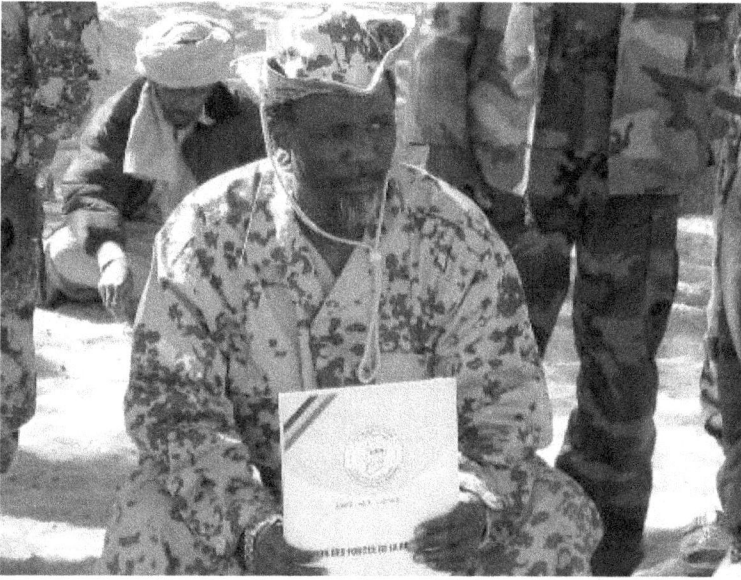

Chadian Insurgent Leader Timane Ardeme of Union of Forces of the Republic

Qatar and Sudan Support for the Overthrow of the Government of Chad

Adding to the volatile security situation in Darfur, a new Chadian rebel group has been organized and is being prepared to launch attacks from Darfur against the government of Chad. This new force is a unification of several Chadian rebel factions under the leadership of Timane Ardeme, who is the cousin of current President Deby of Chad.

Timane Ardeme is the only known person among Chadian politicians to have embraced the Muslim Brotherhood organization and became a member. He was recruited by Sudan's National Congress Party in the 1990s. The Bashir regime in Khartoum helped him with the financial and military assistance of Qatar and Saudi Arabia attempting to overthrow the government of President Deby of Chad. Ardeme organized a rebel movement, which launched a series of attacks between 2006 and 2009 but failed to achieve their objectives. He is among the foreign Muslim Brotherhood leaders who live in Qatar.

Recently, Ardeme, with the support of Sudan and Qatar, united eight Chadian rebel factions under the banner of the insurgent Union of Forces for the Republic. Under his leadership of the new group the objective is to finally achieve the overthrow of the Deby government in Chad.

President Deby of Chad recently declared that Sudan President Bashir backed by his ally Qatar are supporting these rebels planning to destabilize his government. These Chadian rebels are part of the RSF/Janjaweed militias that President Bashir has recruited to commit genocide, war crimes and crimes against humanity in Darfur, South Kordofan and the Blue Nile state. The Union of

Forces for the Republic is currently based in Libya. The *Libya Herald* reported that Sudan with Qatar backing in coordination with the self-declared Islamic State province was fighting the Libyan National Army (LNA) regime of General Khalifa Hafter.

The Bashir regime in turn continues to accuse the LNA of seeking to overthrow his government in Sudan by providing a sanctuary for Darfur resistance fighters.

These Chadian rebels are also part of the estimated 150,000 Mujahideen army that the Sudan government has been organizing since 2016 to overthrow the governments of Libya, Chad and destabilize the Sahel region by establishing an Islamic Caliphate ruled under Islamic Sharia. The unification of Chadian rebel factions is an indication of this strategic objective of President Bashir and his Arab allies.

Chapter Eleven
Sudan hires Washington Lobbyist Firm, Human Rights Advocates and Congress Disputes lifting sanctions

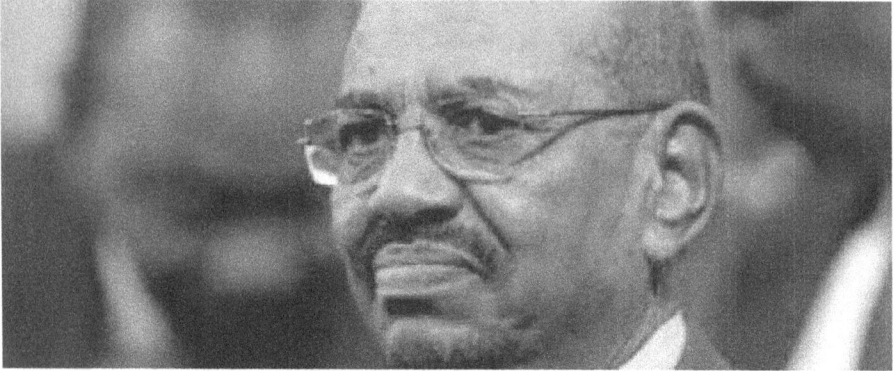

President Omar Hassan al-Bashir of The Republic of the Sudan

On January 13, 2017, former President Obama signed Executive Order No. 13761 temporarily lifting 20-year old sanctions against Sudan led by International Criminal Court indicted war criminal President Omar Hassan al-Bashir. The Executive Order had a look back period of 180 days, which ends on July 12th, whereupon, the Trump Administration might permanently lift sanctions. This comes at a time when new evidence surfaced that a strategic policy group of the Bashir regime in Khartoum continued genocide against the indigenous black African people in Darfur, Nuba Mountains, South Kordofan and the Blue Nile region.

The rancorous dispute between Qatar and four Arab nations, over alleged support for Islamic terrorism and the Muslim Brotherhood, has placed Bashir in a difficult position, as he has been asked by Saudi Arabia to take sides. The government of neighboring Chad issued a statement cutting diplomatic relations with Qatar. Chadian President Idriss Deby has long been waiting for this moment. Qatar has hosted and supported Chadian Islamist groups who have been recruited for Sudan President Omar al-Bashir's Rapid Support Force (RSF)/Janjaweed militias.

In one embarrassing episode in mid-June 2017 General Taha Osman al Hussein, State Minister in the Presidency and Director General of the Presidential Palace in Khartoum, allegedly had been arrested in an failed attempted coup to overthrow President Bashir of Sudan. General al Hussein is a dual Sudan and Saudi Arabia citizen. Subsequent news reports said that General al Hussein and his wife had left the Sudan for Saudi Arabia after he had volunteered to allegedly lead an overthrow of Qatar.

Sudan had initiated an influence campaign in Washington retaining the services of the lobbying firm of Squire Paton Boggs at $40,000 per month to roll back the sanctions permanently. The objective was to make a convincing case that Sudan, despite its terrible human rights record, had nevertheless co-operated in providing useful counterterrorism intelligence on the whereabouts of the notorious Joseph Kony of the Lord's Resistance Army. In fact one of the co-authors, General Abdallah of the Sudan United Movement (SUM), had provided information on Kony's whereabouts to US AFRICOM.

"Will Trump Let a Brutal Dictator off the Hook?"

On June 16, 2017, Greta Van Susteren, host of the former *MSNBC* program *For the Record* aired a segment dealing with the record of human rights violations in the Sudan, "Will Trump Let a Brutal Dictator off the Hook?" Van Susteren had been to the Sudan in the company of Rev. Franklin Graham to view firsthand the conflict and evidence of the Bashir Regime's violations of human rights of indigenous African peoples. Her guests were Ryan Boyette, publisher of the *Nuba Report* and former Virginia Republican Congressman and founding co-chairman of the Congressional Tom Lantos Human Rights Commission.

Boyette, a Florida native, has been in Sudan since 2003 and has a family in the Nuba Mountains. He has covered the six-year war in the Nuba Mountains depicting devastation of the indigenous African people in the region. Despite an alleged truce arranged in January 2017, Boyette said, "nothing has really changed." The Sudan Air force is still dropping barrel bombs from Russian made Antonov cargo planes loaded with shrapnel tearing into civilians. He spoke of no humanitarian access to provide food and medicines leaving starving people resorting to eating leaves and fleeing to caves for safety. This was compounded by a famine and outbreak of cholera in the Sudan. US officials are barred from entering the Nuba Mountains. Boyette is in favor of retaining sanctions. He created a short video of the devastation in the Nuba conflict zone that he has presented in meetings with Congressional human rights leaders.

Former Congressman Wolf, who has been to Sudan seven times, said how can you consider lifting sanctions against the Bashir Regime that has killed more indigenous African people than Islamic terror groups, Al Qaeda, Al Shabab and the Islamic State, combined. Both he and moderator Van Susteren suggested that Washington lobby firm, Squire, Paton Boggs should resign the $40,000 a month retainer with Sudan seeking to permanently lift 20 years of sanctions in light of evidence of continual genocidal ethnic cleansing.

The House Foreign Affairs Committee rebuts recommendation of former US Sudan Envoys

The controversy over lifting Sudan Sanctions rose to a peak in late June 2017, when a noted US Sudan human rights activist Eric Reeves issued a scathing rebuttal letter. It challenged a letter sent to the US House Foreign Affairs Committee by former Special Envoys to Sudan Princeton Lyman and Donald Booth, along with former U.S. Charge d'Affaires in Khartoum, Jerry Lanier, suggesting there was evidence to lift sanctions.

Reeves wrote:

> In this almost three decades of brutal, tyrannical, and serially genocidal rule, this regime has not changed in any significant way. It has certainly not changed in ways claimed as possible by Lyman in December 2011:
>
> > We [the Obama administration] do not want to see the ouster of the [Khartoum] regime, nor regime change. We want to see the regime carrying out reform via constitutional democratic measures." (Interview with *Asharq al-Awsat*, December 3, 2011).
>
> One hardly knows where to begin in parsing the absurdity of this statement, justifying the Obama administration's opposition to regime change. [Regime change] overwhelmingly favored by the vast majority of Sudanese and indeed now the linchpin of political and military opposition to the regime throughout Sudan.

Reeves then proceeded to document the escalation of genocidal ethnic cleansing against the indigenous black African people in Darfur, Nuba Mountains and the Blue Nile region since the Obama Executive Order went into effect.

On June 30, 2017, members of the House Foreign Affairs Committee responded by sending a signed letter to President Trump. It recommended that any decision to lift Sudan sanctions be deferred for at least a year past the July 12th. That would allow a new Special Envoy and team to be appointed and conduct investigations. The letter clearly stated the reasons for their recommendation to the President:

> There has been substantial fighting [by] Sudan in Darfur in recent months, including evidence of targeting civilians by Sudanese armed forces and their affiliated militias. As expected, no humanitarian access has been granted to South Kordofan and Blue Nile states, and only limited access to Darfur.

While the Sudanese government may seem cooperative on counterterrorism efforts, we believe they continue regularly scheduled support for violent non-state armed groups, like the former combatants of the Islamist group, Seleka, the Lord's Resistance Army (LRA). Other similar violent actors [are] operating in Northern and Central Africa, the Middle East and neighboring countries.

As the look back date of July 12th loomed, there were further troubling disclosures.

Was there a failed coup attempt in Khartoum?

The National Congress Party (NCP) regime has been ruling Sudan through deception, intimidation of its opponents and releasing false propaganda through its controlled media. Since June 16, 2017, rumors have spread that General Taha Osman al Hussein, State Minister in the Presidency and the Director General of Presidential Palace, had been arrested in a failed attempted coup to overthrow the genocidal and indicted war criminal President Bashir of Sudan. The media also said that several other senior officers were arrested.

Six of these officers are believed to be from the police corps including the Director General of Sudan's Police force, Hazim Abdelghadir. The Director of Gulf Bank, Omer Ali, and 12 senior members of the NCP were also said to have been arrested.

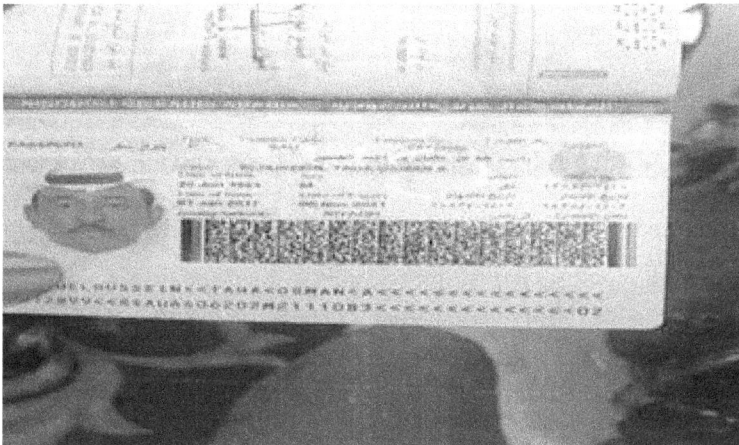

Saudi Passport of General Taha Osman al Husseini

Posted and circulated in media that he was arrested in Khartoum Airport trying to travel abroad

Taha, who is believed to have dual Sudan-Saudi Arabian nationality, was allegedly planning to stage a military coup against President Bashir of Sudan. It was widely circulated among Sudanese social media. It was stated that the coup failed after Taha was arrested at the Khartoum Airport when he was trying to travel aboard with his wife by the security forces that were secretly following his activities including phone calls. In addition to the failed coup, Taha was also accused of passing secret information about Sudan to foreign governments. The rumors also suggested that Taha had secured the support of some foreign leaders to overthrow President Bashir during the Riyadh Islamic conference where Taha was representing President Bashir, who declined to attend. Rumors also suggested that the NCP had split into two groups and President Bashir had been placed under house arrest. The rumors went on saying that the government imposed a curfew in Khartoum and ordered removal of all Rapid Support Force/Janjaweed militias from Khartoum and Kordofan sending them to Darfur.

General Hazim Abdelgadir, Director General of Sudan's Police Force

This picture appeared in the social media that he has been arrested

According to various Sudanese and other social media, Taha was planning a coup with the support of General Mohamed Hamdan Dagolo (Hemetti) the Commander of the Sudan's Rapid Support Forces to overthrow President Bashir. The information about Taha staging a coup in Khartoum, widely circulated in the social media, probably is not true because there is no apparent political tension creating a security situation. It is also evident that there is neither an expulsion of RSF/Janjaweed militias nor imposition of a curfew in the capital of Khartoum.

What is true is that General Taha was relieved from his positions. All other information said on Taha's failed coup are likely to be scenarios developed by Bashir's National Intelligence and Security Services (NISS) agents to draw public attention away from the Qatar-Saudi crisis. It is well known that President

Bashir's regime needs the support of both Qatar and Saudi Arabia governments. Bashir and his regime cannot survive without their support. Bashir also could not take a position supporting either side and leaving the other. Both Qatar and Saudi governments need Bashir's support especially Saudi Arabia because of Bashir's Janjaweed militias supporting Saudis in Yemen war. Qatar is also using President Bashir to train and finance global terrorists such as the groups in Libya, Mali and elsewhere. President Bashir's regime is trying to play the role of mediator despite the fact that Saudi Arabia requested the Sudan regime to clearly choose its position. The issue of Taha's failed coup attempt and arrest is more likely a staged event to draw public attention away from Arab countries' recent crisis with the State of Qatar. Qatar is a major supplier of funding support for the RSF/Janjaweed genocide campaigns in the conflict zones of Darfur, Nuba Mountains and the Blue Nile South Kordofan regions.

The Top Secret Minutes of the Sudan Security Intelligence and Political Committee

Amidst the swirl of events concerning the lifting of sanctions against the Sudan regime of President al-Bashir were stunning revelations contained in the "Top Secret" minutes of The Security Intelligence and Political Committee of Crisis Management held in the Office of the Director of the Sudan National Intelligence and Security Services (NISS) on June 18, 2017. The secret document had been obtained by a reliable informed source and was translated. (see Appendix C)

Attending the Khartoum meeting were the power elite of the reigning National Congress Party (NCP) regime: President Bashir, Vice President Backri Hassan Salih, Foreign Minister Ibrahim Ghandour, Minister of Defense Awad bn Ouf, Hamid Momtaz Secretary of NCP political affairs, and State Minister in the Ministry of foreign affairs, General Mohamed Atta al Mola Director of NISS, General Ibrahim Mohamed al Hassan, Commander of Military Intelligence, Ibrahim Mahamud Vice President of NCP and Professor Ibrahim Ahmed Omer President of Parliament.

The minutes of this Crisis Management Committee revealed the broad sweep of plans for assassination of a major Sudan resistance commander in the Nuba Mountains and senior Officers supporting him. It also addressed sponsorship of international ISIS terrorist activities in the Sahel region of Africa, especially in Libya, and the global Muslim Brotherhood Organization. It elucidated the web of deception in the Bashir regime's influence campaign in Washington, DC, to lift sanctions by the Trump Administration.

These top secret minutes also reflect the Bashir regime's position in the current dispute between Qatar and four Arab Countries: Saudi Arabia, United Arab Emirate, Bahrain and Egypt. It reveals that relations with Iran secretly continue despite the public cutoff in 2015.

The revelations in this NISS document further the case of the letter signed by Members of the US House Foreign Affairs Committee sent to President Trump. The following is a digest of key recommendations of the Sudan NISS Crisis Management Committee at the June 18, 2017 meeting.

Elimination of Nuba Mountains Resistance SPLA/N Commander General Abdalaziz Adam Alhilu

The Committee sought to isolate and eliminate Nuba Mountains SPLA/N Commander General Abdulaziz Adam Alhilu, through use of all government institutions, political, military, intelligence and propaganda. They also will promote Malik Agar, Governor of the Blue Nile State and a leader of the SPLM/N, through an extensive media campaign focusing the African Union's position supporting his legitimacy as SPLM/N head. Allegedly, the Committee minutes contend the South Sudan government does not support Abdulaziz. They would create internal problems for Abdulaziz through tribal conflicts using Nuba people opposing him to foment conflicts inside SPLA/N to weaken and totally destroy it. They indicated that Churches are the main places where communities are gathering in Nuba Mountains and Blue Nile; so they want to use highly trained people to infiltrate into Christian religious communities and create problems for Abdulaziz and SPLM/N. They plan to assassinate officers supporting Abdulaziz using military force through the support of the Agar faction and tribes of Angassana to remove him from the Nuba Mountains.

Recruitment and Infiltration of ISIS fighters to support African and Global Islamic Terrorism

They will continue support for the Global jihad objectives of the Islamic State and the Muslim Brotherhood. To that end they indicated that ISIS fighters in Iraq and Syria were defeated and the desert terrain is not suitable for continued warfare. They would relocate ISIS fighters from Iraq and Syria and infiltrate them into the areas of Bahr al Gazal and Equatorial regions in the South Sudan. The areas of Bahr al Gazal and Equatorial regions would allow ISIS fighters to establish linkage with Boko Haram in Nigeria in the West through the Central African Republic and with Al Shabab of Somalia in the East. They would infiltrate ISIS fighters into neighboring Libya to reinforce ISIS affiliate groups there seeking to defeat the Libyan National Army regime of General Khalifa Haftar to prevent him from attaining power, as they view him as a threat to their regime. They believe that South Sudan President Salva Kiir supports the overthrow of the Khartoum regime, thus they want to overthrow the regime of President Kiir. To that end they would train Southern Sudanese youth, people from West Africa and Nigerian students supporting Boko Haram, as they resemble the South Sudanese Africa tribal people in the capital of Juba. They would infiltrate them into South Sudan as secret agent provocateurs to raise resentment against the regime of President Kiir, seeking its overthrow.

Support for Qatar and Renewal of Iran relations

The Committee minutes indicated that Saudi Arabia is trying to force them to leave Qatar. However, they are not going to leave Qatar because it has been supporting the regime both ideologically and financially. They contend, without the support of Qatar they would have been overthrown and imprisoned. They would reestablish their relations with Iran because of shared Islamic Jihad goals. Qatar, Iran and Turkey have established a relationship which has become a main point of contention raised by the Saudi Arabia and the three other Arab states. As we have written previously, Qatar has provided $200 million under the guise of education reform to Sudan that was diverted to funding the recruitment, training and equipping of more than 24,000 Rapid Support Forces /Janjaweed (RSF) militia. They are under the control of the NISS in 16 camps in the region around Khartoum. These RSF forces were immediately deployed to Darfur and the Nuba Mountains to accelerate the ethnic cleansing of native black African peoples in those conflict zones.

Campaign to influence the Trump Administration's lifting of Sanctions

Prior to the July 12th review by the Trump Administration they allegedly could stop two planned terrorist attacks on American interests in the world to convince Americans of Sudan's seriousness of helping the US in combating global terrorism to justify lifting the sanctions.

They want to prevail on Saudi Arabia and Kuwait to put pressure on the US to lift sanctions. Saudi Arabia had urged President Obama to sign the temporary lifting of Sudan sanctions with his Executive Order. They also think they have co-opted the US Intelligence Community because they understood the way the US intelligence Community think and operate. They contend they have given counterterrorism intelligence information that no other country in the world had given them. In return the US IntelligenceAppendix C Community has very little information about what is happening in Sudan.

This secret document reinforces our earlier contentions based on the captured Arab Coalition Plan. The Bashir regime's objective is to recruit a jihad army of upwards of 150,000 from across the African Sahel region, ISIS Middle East and foreign fighters. The objective is to create a Caliphate ruled under Islamic Sharia law from Khartoum sponsoring global Islamic terrorism in consort with Muslim Brotherhood sponsoring regimes like Qatar and in renewed relations with Shiite Iran. That objective is reflected in the Libyan National Army discovery of documents attesting to the collusion of Sudan, Qatar and Iran in fostering ISIS terrorists seeking to dismantle the Libyan National Army led by General Haftar. Given these secret document revelations, President Trump would be well advised to accept the recommendation in the letter from the US House Foreign Affairs Committee. That would entail deferring consideration of lifting sanctions for at least a year until a new Special Envoy of Sudan and South Sudan is appointed and team assigned to obtain facts that might verify the revelations of the secret June 2017 Sudan Crisis Management Committee minutes. A vital first step would be the appointment of a knowledgeable Special Envoy with plenipotentiary powers to investigate and expose the Bashir regime genocidal jihad objectives. Another would be promoting regime change.

Sudan's diplomatic faux pas denying retention of a DC lobby

Even before President Trump deferred lifting 20-year sanctions against the regime of ICC indicted President Bashir in Khartoum, the lobbying efforts went into action. In early June, news came that the K Street lobby firm, Squire Paton Boggs LLP was retained by the Government of the Republic of Sudan (GRS) on May 23, 2017 at a fee of $40,000 a month. Prominent among the SPB firm members are former Sens. John Breaux (D-La.), Trent Lott (R-Miss.) and former House Speaker John Boehner (R-Ohio). Here is a link to the SPB Foreign Agents Registration Act (FARA).

According to a signed letter, dated May 25, 2017, between SPB and Sudan's Ambassador to the US, His Excellency Maowia Osman Khalid, the scope of work included "a program to: (i) to avoid 'snap back' of U.S. sanctions on Sudan pursuant to Executive Order 13761; and (ii) identify and implement strategies to improve Sudan's investment climate." The SPB FARA was docketed as Registration No. 2165 by the NSD/FARA Registration Unit on May 31, 2017.

The SPB firm members and the Sudan lobbying agreement were promptly blasted by Hollywood actor George Clooney and John Prendergast of the Enough Project in a July 6, 2017 *Time Magazine* op Ed. They wrote:

> Over the last four administrations, Congress has led bipartisan U.S. efforts to isolate the Sudan regime. [...] So it's surprising that Squire Patton Boggs has taken on this account. It's also possible they don't know that the government of Sudan continues to use starvation as a weapon of war on its own people, still funds militias that murder its own innocent civilians, and continues to loot the country of its natural resources and funnel the wealth of Sudan into the hands of regime leaders through massive corruption.

In February 2017, Sudan signed a $300,000 fixed fee contract with Cooke Robotham LLC to advise Sudan on how it could restructure the more than $55 billion in outstanding debt shortly following former President Obama signing Executive Order 13761.

A *Sudan Tribune* headlined a report from Khartoum, "Sudan denies hiring U.S. firms to lobby for lifting of sanctions". It reported State Minister Hamid Mutes saying, "We are a responsible country that does not work through (lobbying) companies, but through the official institutions to end the (economic) embargo imposed on Sudan. We have worked with the official channels in the previous period, we will continue to work in the coming period."

Despite suspension of the Special Committee activities by President Bashir following Trump's signing the deferral order, State Minister Mutes stated in the *Sudan Tribune* report:

> Mutes reiterated that Bashir's decision does not mean to suspend contacts and communications with Washington.
>
> The suspension of the negotiating committee with Washington on lifting sanctions does not mean ending communication adding that contacts will continue through diplomatic and political channels as well as popular efforts of civil society groups, friends and partners.
>
> He called on the foreign affairs committee at the parliament to contribute to repeal the economic embargo on Sudan.
>
> In my meeting with the National Assembly Foreign Affairs Committee, I answered the MPs' questions with all transparency and clarity about the consequences of the postponement, its negative and positive aspects.

The Hill headlined an article, "*Sudan sanctions spur intense lobbying*". It reported:

> The Sudanese were disappointed by Trump's decision to extend a temporary easing of the sanctions, arguing that they had made enough progress on the benchmarks.
>
> Sudanese President Omar al-Bashir ordered the "suspension of the committee that was negotiating [the lifting of the sanctions] with the United States until October 12," according to the official SUNA news agency.
>
> One source told *The Hill* that others in the government are trying to walk back Bashir's comments so that they can work with the U.S. on lifting the sanctions.
>
> It's a posture that may make diplomatic relations between the United States and Sudan difficult moving forward, but there is a sense of optimism among some working on the issue.
>
> "There are decades of mistrust between both governments churning behind all of this. And because of that, the current rapprochement — while striking — is delicate as both sides struggle to build confidence in one another," said the person

familiar with Sudan's advocacy efforts, who emphasized the government is prepared to address its human rights record.

Among the proponents of lifting Sudan sanctions is a former US Special Envoy Princeton Lyman. Lyman, has been criticized for having a questionable relation with the Bashir regime. *The Hill* noted a report authored by a host of former US diplomats and National Security Council experts with the support of *The Atlantic Council*:

> Several former ambassadors and National Security Council officials released an in-depth report for the Atlantic Council arguing that the Sudan sanctions had not worked and that the U.S. government should instead increase diplomatic efforts.
>
> "It doesn't work to say, 'When you've completely changed, we'll lift the sanctions.' It's not the way change comes about," said Princeton Lyman, a former U.S. Special Envoy for Sudan and South Sudan who took part in the Atlantic Council report.
>
> The Atlantic Council held an event in Washington last week to roll out the report.
>
> "We have been waiting for the Sudanese economy to collapse, waiting for [Bashir's government] to fall, waiting for the popular uprising to begin, but it hasn't," said Cameron Hudson, a former aide to Lyman in the Obama administration, during the discussion.

Former US Envoy Lyman's comments may be overblown. *The Sudan Tribune* reported on July 17, 2017:

> Sudan's Minister of Finance, Mohamed Salih al-Rikabi said Khartoum has received a letter from the U.S. Department of Treasury stating the full resumption of financial transactions between Sudan and international banks as of last Thursday.
>
> Al-Rikabi described the U.S. Department of Treasury letter as "significant breakthrough" in Sudan's relations with the international financial sector and international institutions such as the IMF and the World Bank, foreign investors, as well as all Sudanese expatriates whose annual remittances are estimated at $6 billion.

The Wall Street Journal gave no recognition of Finance Minister al-Rikabi's "significant breakthrough" in a story out of Khartoum. However, it did note who is keeping Bashir's rickety economy afloat under the US 20-year sanctions:

> The International Monetary Fund says investments from Persian Gulf states have been critical in keeping this struggling economy

afloat, especially after 2011, when the oil-rich south seceded to become independent South Sudan, taking most of the country's revenue with it.

Pockets of Khartoum are starting to look like Gulf capitals. Skyscrapers bankrolled by Saudi, Kuwaiti and Qatari investments tower over the Blue and White Nile rivers that converge here. One recently developed business and residential district is called Riyadh.

The Saudis had entreated former President Obama to temporarily lift Sudan sanctions against the Bashir regime. Ostensibly, it was allegedly for his cutting off relations with Iran in exchange for billions in *baksheesh* to have the Sudan National Army forces involved in the war against Shia Houthi rebels in Yemen supported by Iran. Problem is Sudan is playing two sides against one another, while pursuing genocidal cleansing of indigenous African people in the conflict zones of Darfur, Nuba Mountains, South Kordofan and the Blue Nile State. An operation involving Mujahideen recruited from the Sahel region of Africa and ISIS fighters from the Middle East funded by Qatar with the ultimate goal of establishing a Caliphate based in Khartoum.

Conclusion

As Alice in Wonderland might have opined about the conundrum of lifting or retaining Sudan sanctions, "curiouser and "curiouser."

Chapter Twelve
President Trump signs order to defer lifting sanctions while rampage continues in Darfur

President Donald Trump signs Executive Order No. 13761 on July 11, 2017

On the evening of July 11, 2017 we received an email from Ken Isaacs of Samaritans Purse containing what appears to be a press statement from the Executive Office of the President Trump indicating that the decision on possible permanently lifting the 20-year sanctions against the Sudan regime of President Omar Hassan al-Bashir may have been deferred from July 12, 2017 to October 12, 2017.

Isaacs sent an email "confirming that this press release came from the White House regarding the President's executive order on the sanctions on Sudan."

On June 30, 2017, the House Foreign Affairs Committee sent a bi-partisan letter to President Trump recommending that he defer any decision on the Sudan sanctions for at least a year to permit the appointment of a new Special Envoy to Sudan and South Sudan and assembly of a team to conduct investigations into the situation and Sudan alleged compliance with the five tracks enumerated in the Executive Order No. 13761.

Below is the text conveyed in Ken Isaacs' email that purports to have been issued by White House:

FOR IMMEDIATE RELEASE

July 11, 2017

EXECUTIVE ORDER
- - - - - - -
ALLOWING ADDITIONAL TIME FOR RECOGNIZING POSITIVE ACTIONS

BY THE GOVERNMENT OF SUDAN AND AMENDING EXECUTIVE ORDER 13761
    By the authority vested in me as President by the Constitution and the laws of the United States of America, including the International Emergency Economic Powers Act (50 U.S.C. 1701 et seq.), the National Emergencies Act (50 U.S.C. 1601 et seq.), the Trade Sanctions Reform and Export Enhancement Act of 2000 (22 U.S.C. 7201-7211), the Comprehensive Peace in Sudan Act of 2004, as amended (Public Law 108-497), the Darfur Peace and Accountability Act of 2006 (Public Law 109?344), and section 301 of title 3, United States Code,

    I, DONALD J. TRUMP, President of the United States of America, in order to take additional steps to address the emergency described in Executive Order 13067 of November 3, 1997, Executive Order 13412 of October 13, 2006, and Executive Order 13761 of January 13, 2017, with respect to the policies and actions of the Government of Sudan, including additional fact-finding and a more comprehensive analysis of the Government of Sudan's actions, hereby order as follows:

    Section 1. Amendments to Executive Order 13761. (a) Section 1 of Executive Order 13761 is hereby amended by striking "July 12, 2017" and inserting in lieu thereof "October 12, 2017".

    (b) Section 10 of Executive Order 13761 is hereby amended by striking "July 12, 2017" and inserting in lieu thereof "October 12, 2017".

    (c) Subsection (b) of section 12 of Executive Order 13761 is hereby amended by striking "July 12, 2017" and inserting in lieu thereof "October 12, 2017".

    (d) Section 11 of Executive Order 13761 is hereby revoked.

Sec. 2. General Provision. This order is not intended to, and does not, create any right or benefit, substantive or procedural, enforceable at law or in equity by any party against the United States, its departments, agencies, or entities, its officers, employees, or agents, or any other person.

DONALD J. TRUMP

THE WHITE HOUSE,
July 11, 2017.

Ryan Boyette
Nuba Report

Sudan Human Rights Advocates on President Trump's Deferral of Lifting Sanctions

Ryan Boyette of the *Nuba Reports* was interviewed by *National Public Radio* just prior to President Trump issuing his Executive Order deferring consideration of permanently lifting the 20-year sanctions against the Bashir regime in Sudan. He commented that the conflict waged by the Khartoum regime against the civilian population in the Nuba Mountains was a "war of attrition against a rebel movement and committing atrocities against civilians."

Further he said, "This is not a small conflict. In the West, we hear of African conflicts and we think of very small arms. The Sudan government has used jet fighters that they are bombing people with. They have tanks and artillery. The SPLA/N rebels also have tanks and artillery. These are big battles."

To illustrate this he had shown a brief video during presentations to Congressional human rights advocates and said "A lot of people have become quite emotional when they watch it."

119

The NPR interviewer noted The U.S. Commission on International Religious Freedom had accused Sudan of demolishing churches and arrested several pastors in recent months and doesn't deserve sanctions relief now.

State Department spokesperson Heather Nauert told reporters that Sudan would retain its designation as a state sponsor of terror.

Dr. Tom Catena 2017 Aurora Prize Awakening Humanity

The *Washington Free Beacon* published an article presenting the views of former Virginia Congressman and founding co-chair of the Congressional Human Rights Caucus Frank Wolf and Catholic Medical Missionary Dr. Tony Catena . Catena had been the recipient of the $1 million Aurora Prize for Awakening Humanity at a ceremony in Erevan, Armenia on May 28, 2017. The Aurora Prize was established to recognize the heroic people combating genocide around the globe.

It is reflective of the Armenian Genocide perpetrated by the Ottoman Turks 102 years ago that killed an estimated 1.5 million victims in razing and rapine of communities and deaths through starvation, forced marches and atrocities directed by the Young Turks.

An *Irish Times* report noted:

Dr. Catena had performed more than 1,000 operations a year using dated or missing medical equipment at the Mother of Mercy Catholic Hospital in the Nuba Mountains while the Bashir rained bombs on the facility. He is the only permanent doctor in the Nuba Mountains, a rugged theatre for battle between the government in Khartoum led by President Omar al-Bashir and rebels from the Sudanese People's Liberation Movement.

Catena commented: "The truth is that after so many years of being dismissed and oppressed the people of Nuba don't trust the government."

Congressman Wolf lauded President Trump's actions in the *Washington Free Beacon* article saying:

> I am very grateful that the administration postponed [sanctions relief] for three months, otherwise they would have been lifting sanctions on a genocidal government, a government that has blood on its hands, and I think that would have been a moral blot in U.S. history,

Catena warned against lifting sanctions saying:

> Any economic benefits resulting from the U.S. lifting sanctions would likely fail to help the civilian population and would instead line the pockets of government officials and military personnel in the capital of Khartoum.

> Any economic improvement in the North would not affect our economic situation here; we're totally cut off from the North. Our fear is an aid boost to the economy in the North will go straight to buying more weapons or providing more money for government forces to pay for military needs.

To emphasize the point, Catena said, "More aid will go for weapons."

SEPTEMBER 9, 2015

"Men With No Mercy"

Rapid Support Forces Attacks against Civilians in Darfur, Sudan

Available In العربية | English

In the wake of the Trump Administration Executive Order on July 11, deferring a decision to permanently lift the 20-year sanctions against the regime of ICC indicted war criminal Sudan President Bashir there was evidence of violations of two of the five tracks included in the original Obama Executive Order No. Executive Order No. 13761 of January 13, 2017.

First, was the brutal ejection by the Rapid Support Forces/Janjaweed militia (RSF/Janjaweed) of Darfur university students on a protest march. Second, were actions by the RSF/Janjaweed against several communities across Darfur. Third, was further evidence of Sudan providing a base for the overthrow of the regimes of President Idriss Deby of Chad and the Libyan National Army (LNA) regime of Field Marshall Khalifa Hafter in Tripoli. The objective of the Bashir regime is to destabilize Northern and Central Africa creating a caliphate ruled under Islamic Sharia law from Khartoum

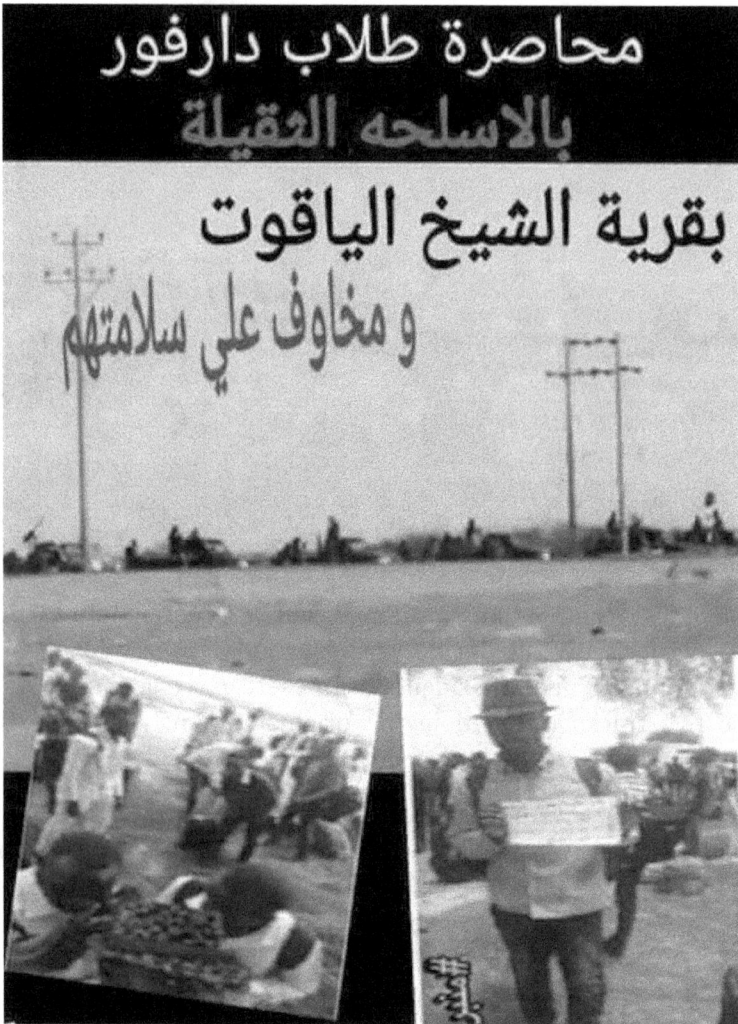

محاصرة طلاب دارفور
بالاسلحه الثقيلة

بقرية الشيخ الياقوت
و مخاوف على سلامتهم

Darfurian university students surrounded at the village of Sheik al Yagoot
in Sudan, July 20, 2017
The translated note reads "With heavy weapons/ in the village of Sheik al Yagoot/
fearing for their safety."

Protest March of Darfur students ejected from Sudan State University

Amnesty International (*AI*) protested the forced ejection of more 1,000 Darfur students who resigned from Bakht al-Ruda University in Duwem in the White Nile State, located 190 kilometers from Khartoum. The students resigned because of discrimination they were facing at the University.

They were prevented by the National Intelligence and Security Service (NISS) from traveling on buses to the capital of Khartoum to deliver their protests. The problem started on July 18, 2017 when the University Administration dismissed 50 Darfur students in this year alone. They were protesting the false arrest and dismiss of 14 of their colleagues for allegedly accused of killing 2 police officers.

123

The NISS agents banned the commercial bus system in Duwem from transporting the Darfur students. The students decided to walk the 190 kilometers to Khartoum. They marched 17 kilometers from Duwem and arrived at Sheik al Yagoot village where the NISS RSF/Janjaweed units, who prevented them from continuing their journey to Khartoum, stopped them. The Sheik al Yagoot village chief had provided them with food and water during the ordeal.

As events unfolded, the protesting students were surrounded by 17 RSF/Janjaweed heavily armed Toyota Pickup trucks or 'technicals,' and placed on buses the regime had arranged to transport them back to Darfur. The students eventually arrived in al Fashir, the capital of North Darfur on July 24, 2017.

The *AI* reported:

> The Sudanese authorities must end the continued discrimination of Darfuri students at universities [...] as more than 1,000 Darfuri students of Bakht al-Ruda University [in Duwem] in the White Nile State, [located 190 kilometers] from the capital Khartoum. They were seeking to demand the release of 10 of their colleagues, accused of killing two police officers.

> The students are now blockaded on the southern edge of the capital Khartoum, after NISS agents from delivering a statement listing their demands to the government stopped them. They also want 14 other colleagues who were expelled from the university readmitted. Instead of stopping them, the authorities should protect them and ensure that their grievances are heard.

> "These students only want to present a petition to their leaders, but instead of helping and protecting them, the NISS have chosen to block them, in callous disregard of their rights to freedom of expression and peaceful assembly," said Mutton Waynoka, Amnesty International's Regional Director for East Africa, the Horn and the Great Lakes.

> "Instead of stopping them, the authorities should protect them and ensure that their grievances are heard."

> The two policemen were killed on 9 May as they violently broke up clashes between ruling party and opposition students over disputed guild elections. Seventy students were arrested that day, all of them Darfuri. Investigations into the policemen's deaths are still underway.

Note this excerpt from an article about the history of Bakht al-Ruda University by Darfur human rights advocate Juma al Wakhil, "Discrimination Conflicts in Sudanese Universities against Darfur Students."

The Bakht al Ruda institute is well known to train teachers. It was the first institute established in the Sudan to educate teachers. However, following the 1989 military coup the Bashir regime changed some of the Sudanese civil society institutions into Mujihadeen training camps. For instance, the Senior Secondary Schools of Ghor Tagat and Hantub were changed into Mujahideen training bases. Osama bin Laden and other terrorists received trained on those bases. The regime destroyed the educational system that formerly existed in Sudan by burning books at Khartoum University. They destroyed the knowledge resources that educated people. Bakht al Ruda was changed from an institution training teachers into an institution training terrorists, such as the current Director of the University.

RSF/Janjaweed Militia Rampage and resettlement of foreign recruits in Darfur

The forced ejection of Darfur university protest marchers by the RSF/Janjaweed was one example of the oppression of the Darfur people by the Bashir regime since the Trump sanctions deferral order was issued. President Bashir plans on mobilizing all government militias including the Border Guard Janjaweed militias commanded by Musa Hilal and integrate them into the RSF/Janjaweed militias. Two months ago RSF/Janjaweed families were transported from Chad and Niger and initially deployed in Geneina, the capital of the Western Darfur region. They were then moved by large trucks from Geneina to establish new villages around Gallab Mountain near Tabit, not far from al Fashir, the capital of North Darfur. On their arrival, the Khartoum regime delivered aid from al Fashir to help settle the new arrivals.

There has been increase in rampages by the RSF/Janjaweed militias throughout Darfur seeking to intimidate and ethnically cleanse the indigenous black African people from the region.

Beside looting and expropriation of property, kidnapping and ransom for release of hostages have become sources of funding and income for RSF/Janjaweed militias. As examples there were reports of forced ejection from villages, torture, killing, and kidnapping for ransom in Kas, South Darfur and in Eastern Jebel Marra. A trader was kidnapped from Kas and taken to an RSF/ Janjaweed base near the town and security forces refused to go and release the man. Villagers were also kidnapped in the Katur area in Eastern Jebel Marra and their whereabouts are still unknown.

On July 22, 2017 ten people are killed in tribal clashes between Ma'alia and Rezeigat in Eastern Darfur region and the fighting is continuing. Both tribes are equipped with government supplied arms and trucks. Another group of RSF/Janjaweed militia riding horses and camels attacked farmers on their farms in the area of Hejair Tono. The militia force shot and killed five people and injured six others, some of who were seriously wounded. According to Hisein Abu Sharati, the Coordinator of the Internally Displaced Persons in Darfur interviewed on *Radio Dabanga* on July 24, 2017, the RSF/Janjaweed militias have displaced over 500,000 people currently residing in the Kalma and Salam IDPs camps surrounding Niyala. The newly displaced people are living the in open and no one is providing them with humanitarian assistance.

The RSF/Janjaweed militias are prohibiting villagers of Tabit and Taweela from cultivating their land.

Darfurians have no venue to bring complaints about their grievances or obtain justice in Sudan.

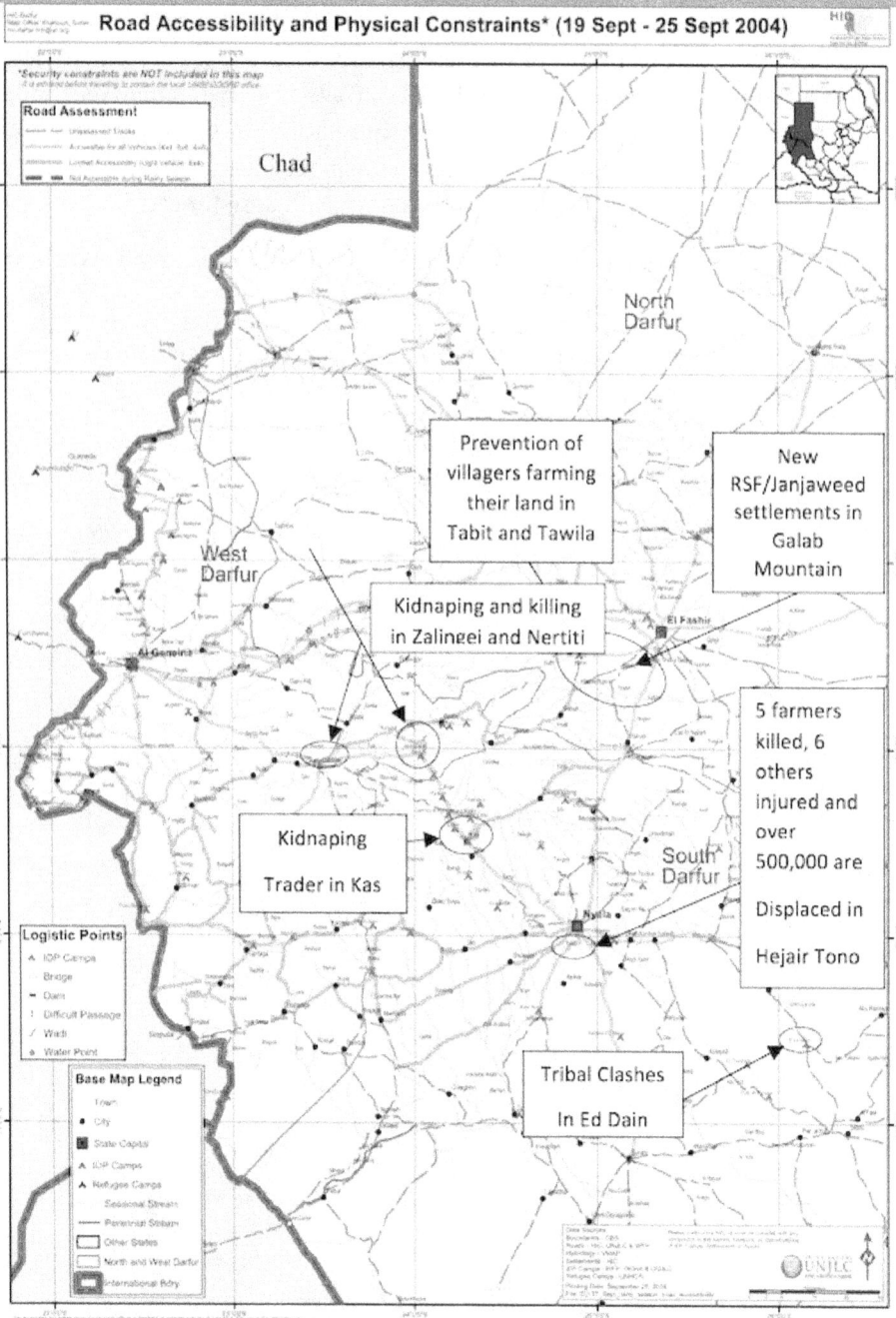

Map of Darfur, Sudan in the boxes on the map are incidents mentioned in this chapter

Chapter Thirteen
Could a $7.3 Billion Federal Appellate decision against Sudan for 1998 African Embassies upset Sanction Relief

US Embassy Blast, Nairobi, Kenya, August 8, 1998

On Friday, July 28, 2017 the US Federal Appellate Court in Washington in a ruling affirmed a District of Columbia Appellate Court ruling granting an award of $7.3 billion against Sudan compensating US and potentially non-US African victims in the 1998 Al Qaeda bombings that destroyed two US Embassies in the east African nations of Kenya and Tanzania. The Federal Appellate court ruling came near the 19th anniversary on August 8, 1998 of the "simultaneous bombing at US embassies in Nairobi, Kenya and Dar es Salaam, Tanzania, killing 224 people. More than 5,000 are wounded. Twelve of those killed in Kenya were US citizens." Sudan and Iran had been implicated in providing sanctuary and funding training bases for Osama bin Laden and Al Qaeda terrorists, 12 of who were indicted. Sudan continued funding al Qaeda, after the alleged departure of Bin Laden in 1996.

These attacks were allegedly retribution by al Qaeda for US coalition forces "despoiling the holy lands" of Saudi Arabia during the First Gulf War in Kuwait against the regime of the late Iraqi strongman Saddam Hussein. The African Embassies bombings followed a similar revenge truck bombing at Khobar Towers on June 25, 1996 that were grounds for Bin Laden allegedly departing the Sudan. The Khobar, Saudi Arabia bombing was perpetrated by Iran and proxy Hezbollah's terrorist mastermind Imad Mughniyah. 19 US service men and one Saudi national were killed, and 498 other nationalities were wounded. A 2006 US federal court case had found Iran and Hezbollah guilty of perpetrating the blast.

The Federal Appellate Court decision in Washington on Friday came amidst the Trump Administration review of the Obama Administration Executive Order No. 13761 signed on January 13, 2017 temporarily lifting the 20-year sanctions against the regime of ICC-indicted Sudan President Omar Hassan al-Bashir. President Trump signed an executive order on July 11, 2017 deferring a decision on permanently lifting the Sudan sanctions until October 12, 2017. How this federal Court ruling will materially impact on the ultimate Trump Administration decision is a matter of speculation. Further, it might complicate possible recent permission granted the Khartoum regime by the US Treasury that allegedly may enable Sudan to use the international financial transaction system.

The Hill reported on the background and outstanding implementation questions that now face the DC Appellate court regarding compensation of American and non-US victims, "Court upholds $7.3B judgment against Sudan over embassy bombings."

> A federal appeals court on Friday ordered Sudan to pay more than $7 billion in damages to American families of victims of the 1998 embassy bombings in Africa.
>
> The U.S. Court of Appeals for the D.C. Circuit upheld a lower court ruling that Sudan had liability for the bombings at U.S. embassies in Nairobi, Kenya, and Dar es Salaam, Tanzania.
>
> However, it threw out the $4.3 billion in punitive damages and is seeking to clarify whether the non-American victims' families qualify for a chunk of the more than $7.3 billion in damages.
>
> The ruling, written by Judge Douglas Ginsburg, a Reagan appointee, affirmed much of the lower courts' ruling and rejected arguments from Sudan's government that the court had considered "inadmissible evidence" to make their final determination.
>
> "We're obviously very pleased that the D.C. Circuit has affirmed [a lower court] decision after what has been a long struggle in court of the families," said Stuart Newberger, a lawyer for the U.S.

families at law firm Crowell & Moring. "We are hopeful that with this ruling, the Americans who were killed in [the attacks] get closer to reaching a final resolution to the tragic saga in their lives and finally get some closure."

Lawyers for the Sudanese government argued that the entire case should have been thrown out for several reasons, foremost by challenging the court's interpretation of the Foreign Sovereign Immunity Act (FSIA), which was revised in the middle of the 15-year legal proceeding.

Osama bin Laden lived in Sudan until the government kicked him out in 1996. The court took the side of expert witnesses that said the country continued to fund the terrorist group al Qaeda, which carried out the attacks that killed 200 people — including 12 Americans.

Sudan has denied its responsibility, saying that it tried to offer bin Laden to the U.S.

The federal appeals court is now asking the D.C. Court of Appeals, the top local court in the District of Columbia, if the families of non-American victims are eligible for compensation, because those provisions fall under state and not federal laws.

The ruling comes against the background of increased lobbying by both the American family members and the Sudanese government, which is working to lift U.S. sanctions.

The victims this week hired a lobbying firm, Kamins Consulting, to help obtain compensation for U.S. government workers injured or killed in the attacks in Kenya and Tanzania.

Scott Kamins has worked at both the Republican National Committee (RNC), where he served as its liaison to Capitol Hill, and at the State Department in the George W. Bush administration.

They also have Monument Policy Group, Morris J. Amitay — who worked as a Foreign Service Officer at the State Department from 1962 to 1969 — and McGuire Woods Consulting.

The firms are working to keep and expand a program that provides money to any American victim of terror attacks who also "have a federal judgment of liability and a separate judgment for a damage award," said Frank Donatelli of McGuire Woods, who works on the account.

Previous attempts to set up a fund for the victims proved unsuccessful, but lobbyists eventually were able to tuck a provision into an update to a law that pays for healthcare for 9/11 first responders.

It put billions of dollars into an account with money obtained from fines paid by a French bank that violated sanctions levied against Sudan, Cuba and Iran. It also set aside $1 billion for the victims of the U.S. embassy bombings. Earlier this year, those families collected a total of $230 million.

"If they're going to have access to our financial system, part of the removal of the sanctions should involve compensating American victims of terror that they've been found liable for harming," Donatelli said.

Donatelli said that paying the reparations would likely improve diplomatic relations with the U.S. and pave the way for lifting sanctions on Sudan.

The lobbying firms on retainer, which hadn't yet been paid by the families, received contingency fees for the successful effort. The three firms made about $600,000 each for two years of work.

Meanwhile, Sudan recently hired Squire Patton Boggs to advocate on its behalf with executive branch officials and Congress on improving relations with the U.S. — including lifting sanctions and paving the way for an increase in foreign investment.

It also has boutique law firm Cooke Robotham on retainer.

"We're hopeful the government of Sudan will continue to engage in a way that will allow them to finally close the door on their terrorist past and rejoin the family of civilized nations in every respect," said Newberger, who is not acting as a lobbyist for the families.

Chapter Fourteen
Sudan President Bashir's 'disarmament' plan in Darfur is cover for Genocide

The Second Vice-President of Sudan Hasabo Mohamed Abderhaman

The Second Vice-President of Sudan Hasabo Mohamed Abderhaman met with the five Governors of Darfur and the so-called Higher Commission for the Collection of Unlicensed Firearms and Vehicles on August 7, 2017 in El Fashir, the capital city of North Darfur. He stated that he was carrying out a campaign of disarmament to establish government authority in the region. The Vice-President also visited four other Darfur regions - Central, Southern, Western and Eastern Darfur pushing his campaign of disarming civilians. Hasabo said on *Radio Dabanga*, "As of today, we will not allow arms to be in the hands of civilians under any pretext, other than the regular forces". He gave firm instructions to security forces comprised of Rapid Support Forces (RSF), Border Guards, Popular Defense Forces, Desert Shield (Janjaweed) and Sudanese Armed Forces to disarm Darfur civilians.

This campaign contradicts the fact that Darfurian civilians have no arms that the Vice-President's Security forces could disarm. Abderhaman should ask himself why he falsely accuses innocent and helpless Darfur civilians of possessing arms. How long do President Bashir and his regime think they can continually deceive the public and the international community?

Since 1986, the Sudan regime has launched similar campaigns against the people of Darfur. The results speak for themselves. There has been no establishment of peace under the regime's authority in the region. Instead, disarming Darfur civilians has been the cover for the Bashir regime to harass villagers and arrest activists. It purposefully sent messages to confuse the public and the international community that the government is making efforts to bring peace and stability. In reality the regime is organizing and arming more Arab tribal militias. They began arming Arab tribes in 1986. Subsequently, these Arab tribal militias continued to attack indigenous peoples' villages. The entire Arab population of Darfur, including those the regime brought from Chad, Mali, Mauritania, Central African Republic (CAR) and elsewhere are considered part of the regime's security apparatus. They are the only ones authorized by the regime to carry weapons and own vehicles that the Vice-President talked about during the *Radio Dabanga* broadcast. Someone should ask the Vice-President how he could disarm Darfur civilians of arms and vehicles that they do not possess.

Approximately 5 million of the estimated 12 million Darfurian population is internally displaced. The majority of them live in more than 65 internally displaced person camps; others have migrated to major cities inside Sudan or have become residents in UN High Commission for Refugees (UNHCR) camps in neighboring countries. In Chad in 2017, there are about 317,219 Darfurians living in UNHCR camps. About the same number live in Chad outside UN camps. 2,000 Darfurians live in Bambari and Sam UN refugee camps in CAR, an equivalent number live in Kenyan UNHCR camps. These are not the only countries where Darfurian people have sought refuge. There are about 600 living in UN refugee camps in Ghana. That leaves out ex-patriate Darfurians living in South Sudan, Egypt, Israel, Libya, Europe, United States and Canada. Those who remain inside Darfur are targeted in raids by the RSF/Janjaweed militia that continually carry out genocidal ethnic cleansing actions killing, displacing, seizing properties and occupying land of this unarmed population.

The Bashir regime secretly armed Arab tribes they brought into Darfur who have been integrated into RSF/Janjaweed militia units. They conduct a veritable "scorched earth ethnic cleansing campaign" burning villages, scattering and killing residents and stealing animals. The Arab tribal Janjaweed militia's threatening behavior causes residents to reconsider defending their villages. At this stage very few people are aware of the regime's strategy using Arabs for ethnic cleansing in Darfur. When the indigenous Darfurian people discovered the conspiracy and complained to the government about arming the Arabs, the authorities denied it saying that they gave Arabs weapons under the pretext of defending their animals from thieves in the remote areas where they usually go looking for pastures. However, the government failed to convince the villagers.

Display of weapons collected in fake Sudan 'disarmament' campaign in Darfur

To cover up these crimes, they began distributing a few weapons to some village heads to defend their villages. That was immediately followed by a duplicitous disarmament campaign. The Sudan government introduced the disarmament campaign in 1987 to conceal its crimes creating the Arab tribal militias and providing them with special protection. Despite several disarmament campaigns the government has launched since the1980s no Arab or Arab militias have been disarmed of their weapons. Instead, they are armed and supplied with money and logistics.

The regime typically deploys large military forces to disarm villagers and at the same time conduct conscription. While disarming villages of weapons that regime authorities gave them; the army also rounds up youths and sends them to military training camps in Khartoum. Following training and equipping them, the regime deploys them in Sudan Army units to fight SPLA in the South Sudan, Nuba Mountains and the Blue Nile state. As soon as the military carries out disarmament operations in villages, reclaiming weapons and conscripting youths, Arab militias launch attacks on the undefended. This tactic is used by the Bashir government to force Darfuri youths into the Sudan Army to fight the SPLA. Moreover, at the same time it enables Arab militia to attack undefended villages, kill and displace residents, ultimately seizing their properties.

Originally, these Arab Janjaweed militia raids and pogroms were carried out using horses and camels. The militias would seize everything that they could carry burning what was left. At this stage, the regime was distributing AK-47 assault rifles. This tactic gradually transitioned from using animals as transport into supplying these Janjaweed militias with Toyota pickup trucks equipped with heavy machine guns and mortars backed by Sudanese Air Force.

Between 1993 and 1996, Osama Bin Laden also supplied herds of camels and cattle to the families of Janjaweed militias in Waddi Salih, Western Darfur region. He visited Waddi Salih and planned to establish training camps for al Qaeda. But he left Sudan prior to beginning that phase. The communication towers he built are still standing in Sarira Mountains, Western Darfur Region.

In 1996 the strategy of faux disarmament was clearly evident especially in the Western Darfur Region. The Army conducted large-scale disarmament operations while Janjaweed militias launched attacks, burnt villages and displaced more than 2,000 people from the Western Darfur Region but failed in these campaigns. The Khartoum government began supporting them with government ground and air forces. That enabled the regime to bring more Arabs from Chad and organize them into militias. This forced the indigenous Darfurian people to form the two resistance movements: The Sudan Liberation Movement [SLM] and Justice and Equality Movement [JEM] in 2003, to defend their rights.

The Bashir regime in Khartoum recruited Arabs using this tactic for years to ethnically cleanse Darfur of its indigenous black African people and occupy the land. The truth is that Darfur civilians had little to no weapons. The regime distributed such weapons to Arabs for several years. Therefore, there is a need to disarm Arab tribal militias not Darfurian civilians.

The weapons and vehicles that Sudan Vice-President Hasabo was talking about were part of Janjaweed militias that refused to support government plans to join RSF militias and kill Darfurian people. Others refused to go to Yemen to fight for Saudi Arabia, especially those Janjaweed militias that are operating under the command of Musa Hilal. In 2016, he refused to execute government orders because the regime failed to implement an agreement he concluded with it in al Geneina, the capital of the Western Darfur region in July 2015. Under that agreement, he was to be promoted to the rank of Major General, allowing him to recruit 10,000 for his militia force. He was promised 10 billion Sudanese pounds and was to be given command of all Janjaweed militias in Darfur. President Bashir is notorious for not honoring deals he signs with his opponents.

Instead of Hilal, Bashir created an RSF/Janjaweed militia and nominated Mohamed Hamdan Dagolo (Hemetti) who was Chadian by origin as commander. Musa Hilal, the notorious Janjaweed commander whose militias killed thousands of people and burned hundreds of villages, especially in North Darfur, was hoping to be given that command.

The fact is "disarmament" in Darfur is completely fictitious, as those who possessed arms and Toyota pickup trucks in Darfur are government militias. They are the armed RSF/Janjaweed militias that create insecurity and instability for Darfurians. Vice President Hasabo knows well that those who own weapons and vehicles are his Arab tribal militias, not the indigenous Darfurians.

Harun Mediger, a member of Musa Hilal's militia told *Radio Dabanga* on August 11, 2017 that Vice-President Hasabo's "disarmament campaign" is clearly targeting Sheik Musa Hilal and his Border Guard militias. He wants to integrate these militias into the RSF, but this will not happen. It is clear that the Bashir regime's objective is not to make peace in Darfur but to mobilize more Arab militias and integrate them into RSF in order to commit more atrocities in Darfur, Nuba Muntains and Blue Nile conflict regions. Bashir's ultimate objective raising this RSF/Janjaweed militia is to destabilize governments of the neighboring countries of Chad, Libya and CAR.

Many Darfurian activists ignored the announcement of Hasabo's "disarmament campaign." One Darfurian activist, who remained anonymous, told *Radio Dabanga* on August 7, 2017, "All those who carry arms in Darfur mostly belong to militias backed by the government, supported with weapons, and they are called many names such as Rapid Support Forces or Border Guards." He also insisted that the process of disarmament in Darfur "does not require a lot of talking." These "weapons can be collected by the leaders of these militias," Hissein Abu Sharati, the Coordinator of Darfur IDP camps said. He, also, told Radio Dabanga,"Government announcements to collect weapons misleads local and international public opinions."

Conclusion

The Bashir regime has continually for decades carried out an Orwellian campaign of 'disarmament' in Darfur as cover for genocidal ethnic cleaning of indigenous black African people. It has recruited Arab tribes who conduct these operations and are the only people in Darfur allowed by Bashir's regime to possess arms and Toyota pickup trucks. They are considered by the regime as an integral part of the government security forces and therefore are immune from prosecution. They commit wide-ranging atrocities against the indigenous black African Darfurian population that the Bashir Arab regime in Khartoum wants to exterminate and occupy their land. This Arab RSF/Janjaweed militia carries out genocide in Darfur under the direct control of Sudan's National Intelligence and Security Services (NISS) that organizes, trains, arms, and supports logistically committing atrocities against innocent indigenous black African civilians.

Chapter Fifteen
Don't believe your lying eyes: Bashir's deception strategy

President Omar Ahmad Hassan al-Bashir of The Republic of the Sudan

In this volume the authors have presented evidence and discussion of the stance of the Republic of the Sudan. The regime of Omar al-Bashir has undertaken an age-old struggle to institute an Islamic State in Sudan spreading it across the Sahel. According to his speeches with no western media present in the last year, he explains that black Africans have no place in such a state and must be chased out, killed or enslaved as in Mauritania. This stance presents a problem that has been obfuscated by negotiators and diplomats alike as they try to bring peace to this troubled area, when Bashir does not want peace, but does want control.

Ambassador Princeton Lyman of the U.S. Peace Institute in Washington, DC articulated the US position on Sudan in Testimony Before the House Foreign Affairs Subcommittee on Africa, Global Health, and Global Human Rights & International Organizations on April 26, 2017. As we compare that speech to the agenda of Khartoum presented in this volume and two leaked documents presented by Eric Reeves, it becomes clear how the wheels of progress toward agreement and peace are bogged down. The negotiations have created a stage with many players but a negotiation team that is only looking at two players, 'rebel' versus 'Government'. It is an admirable goal to try to play a multi-dimensional chess game in two dimensions, but it really can only happen, if you can see the whole board and all its pieces. The nature of Khartoum, the nature of the opposition, the ethos of the US, the external forces are each multifaceted.

'Change the face' Game

Sudan has many faces and the Bashir regime plays from face-to-face for the benefit of his sovereign government and its vision. This "change the face" policy allows them to stay in control by changing which face they present to the world.

Sovereignty

Sudan is playing a sovereignty face to the US. They claim they are the 'duly elected government' and a sovereign nation under UN rules. The rebels, then, are 'terrorists and insurgents' against the government, which is what Bashir called them in graduation speeches in Khartoum last May 2017 for over 11,000 mujahideen. The government is asking the US to help solve this 'rebel problem' by encouraging unification under the present government. Lyman, in his testimony, is following the Bashir regime line; when he points out that the rebels just need to accept the government as it is. The requirement of the rebels to accept the government's offer is that they give up their arms. This would leave them exposed to the secret plan of the Bashir government, presented in Appendix B, to rid the country of black indigenous people and replace them with Arab tribes, replacement which is never brought up in these negotiations. The assumption that the Government will not 'sign an agreement and then attack again' is also not clear given the number of regime originated cease fires that have been quickly broken by the government itself (e.g. 16 in 2016 alone and none broken by the 'rebels'). Just accepting the sovereign Sudanese government 'as it is' could be a deadly risk to the resistance who might sign such an agreement. That was the point raised by SPLM Darfur resistance leader Abdel Wahid al-Nour in Chapter Two when he challenged US Special Envoy Donald Booth. Both the commitment to 'rid and replace' and the risk of that commitment being no guarantee of peace seem to be Ignored by US officials.

Omar al Bashir calls the resistance "terrorists"at graduation May 11,2017

Fighter of Terrorism

Ambassador Princeton N. Lyman former Special Envoy to The Republic of the Sudan and to the Republic of South Sudan

Lyman in his US House Subcommittee testimony also pointed to the cause of breakdown in negotiations, the alleged instability of the resistance movements. Instability perpetrated by Bashir's Generals who gloated in 2014 about using secret provocateurs to undermine and create suspicions among every resistance movement. These Generals were proud of their psychological warfare achievements. Note these comments:

> They must be divided in the same way the movement in the South was divided. We have studied the psychological tendencies of the SPLM cadres and leadership, also the movement locations and the division of the active and educated cadres and those with tribal dimensions. We made lists of the vertical and horizontal relationships between the cadres of these movements. This will help us launch a psychological campaign of rumors against them to see that, they got divided like the SPLM in the South. -General Al-Rashiid Faqiri, Director of National Security (2014).

The sovereignty of the government of Sudan led them to believe that it is acceptable to launch a psychological attack to destroy their opposition. There would be no need to do this, if the goal was to work with them. The fear of the government falling compels Bashir and his National Congress Party government to act strongly and violently to eradicate the resistance. Bashir's Generals are clear on their stance:

> These are all conspiracies aiming at dismantling the rule of the National Salvation Revolution and sentencing its' leaders to be hanged. Facing reality is important. Even the Addis meeting went in the same direction of defaming the Islamic Movement and was an attempt to impose conditions they couldn't achieve through

fighting.   -Major General Hashim Osman Al-Hussein, Director General of Police (2014)

There is no intention of cooperation with those who do not share the Islamic Revolution Vision. Yet, Lyman holds to the tenet that this regime wants pathways to peace, inclusiveness, democracy, and respect for human rights, when behind closed doors they are maneuvering ways to block all of those.

Lyman also states that the US needs to develop relationships with the rebel groups, which implies the US has not. If the US intends a win-win game that requires a spirit of cooperation. The US would need to find out what a 'win' is for the rebels and the government. Khartoum has stated that they only want an Islamic state that is allowed to work toward cleansing the land by following the objective of the Arab Coalition Plan in Appendix B saying, "Whenever there is an opportunity kill them." Such rhetoric does not leave much room for both sides to win or cooperate. Lyman's goal to produce a win-win solution requires that the US truly know both sides. In the case of the rebels, he bemoans his lack of relationship with the Sudan resistance. Meanwhile, the Sudan Government says:

> Even those who came during the days of Naivasha went without knowing how we think or work. -Major General Mohammed Atta, Director General of N.I.S.S in 2014.

Instead of doing his homework, Lyman in his Congressional testimony and in other declarations calls the situation "complex or complicated."

Bashir's Sudan regime envisions an Islamic State that does not include the majority of indigenous people in the country, while the rebels envision an inclusive government that allows everyone to be involved without his Islamic Revolutionary agenda. In the National Political Crisis Committee minutes of June 2017 in Appendix C, Bashir's regime makes it very clear there is no intention of cooperation. There is only deception to fool the US into lifting the sanctions, so they can do what they want freely. General Mohamed Atta al Mola said after addressing all the actions Sudan will do to get the US sanctions lifted:

> Let's be ready to face the period after the lifting of sanctions because we will be a free country (to) determine our relations and no one can dictate to us what to do.

Lyman grants that Bashir is the leader of a sovereign nation, but he has misunderstood the underlying goal spoken behind closed doors, which would bring one to conclude there indeed is no "crack in the door" for peace, as Lyman offered.

Needy

Sudan also presents a face to the US of being a needy recipient of aid. They present themselves as a poor nation who cannot take care of its people (and there are many hungry people.) In actuality, they are doing business in many countries in weapons and military production items, as well as, shipping food and other commodities like gum arabic to the highest bidder. Sudan prides itself on its gold production and is concerned about protecting those assets according to General Atta in minutes of the 2014 secret meetings. Behind closed doors he said:

> The military industries will cover all our needs in the armed forces. You must know that we have around forty (40) companies abroad that constitute the investments for security purposes in addition to the Islamic Movement companies, and Public Security companies whose total capital is greater than two billion. -General Abd al-Rahim Mohammed Husein, Minister of Defense

The discussion continues that all this investment was planned, as they felt they needed a cover due to possible targeting. So that when their Islamic State plan became known they would have businesses out of the country to be in place as an income cushion. The plan included finishing off the indigenous African people and then using the money from that effort to bolster the economy. In this volume, it is very clear that Sudan has for many years gotten abundant gifts and aid from wealthy Arab states and monarchies as depicted in Chapter Six. Yet, they still seek help from the US.

Lyman in his April 2017 Congressional testimony offered a USAID rescue plan for Sudan, while the regime boasts of its hidden assets, financial stability and preparedness. Lifting the 20-year US sanctions is important to the regime because it limits Sudan's ability to access those out of country financial reserves. As is discussed in Chapter Thirteen, the US Treasury Department opened up Sudan access to the international financial transactions system following President Trump's signing his executive order deferring permanently lifting sanctions until October 12, 2017. A needy Sudan is a disguise used as a fundraiser for the Bashir regime to complete genocidal ethnic cleansing of indigenous black African peoples and prepares the way for an Islamic conquest of the Sahel region of Africa.

Helpful

Another face the Sudan presents to the US is 'helpful.' They say they are helping us in the war on terror. Sudan is in a position in the Arab world in which they are friends with all Islamic nations. Dr. Hassan al Turabi of Sudan helped to found meetings of all Islamic nations originally called The Organization of Islamic Conference in 1969 and are now called Organization of Islamic Cooperation

[OIC]. Sudan maintains a working relationship with Islamic sectarian bitter enemies like Iran and Saudi Arabia. That strategy also extends to Islamic extremist groups like Nigeria's Boko Haram, Al Qaeda and the Islamic State. Sudan is thus able to tell the US they can obtain intelligence on all of these extremist Islamic terrorist actors on the world stage. Meanwhile, behind closed doors, as revealed in the secret June 2017 National Political Crisis Committee in Appendix B, the Bashir regime explains that they limit the information passed to the US government and plan to create false events that throw the US off the trail of terrorism. The Bashir regime knows that using traditional surveillance networks is rather ineffective in this changing jihadist movement environment. 'Counterintelligence helpfulness' is listed as one of the five tracks required by the US to lift the sanctions. The US, according to Lyman, mistakenly thinks the present relationship has been very helpful. No wonder help for the resistance is slim and genocide is invisible under the negotiating table.

Moderate face versus radical reality

Sudan is a radical Sufi Islamist State. Some say it is majority Sunni, but most who practice do not hold to traditional Sunni rites. Wikipedia says,

> A great majority of Muslims in Sudan adhere to Sufism or are heavily influenced by it, making Sudan one of the most tolerant Muslim majority countries in the world.

Unlike other Islamic States, Sudan is tolerant of all international and national Islamic movements, who believe that the world should be ruled by Sharia Law. The Generals' meeting 2014 explained:

> We are the only country in the world that will not be affected by the conflicts taking place between Sunni Islamic groups and the Shia. We have succeeded in maintaining good relations with all Islamic groups, through the cover of social organizations, and not through the state institutions. The secret of the strength of the National Salvation Revolution (NCP) Government lies in the smooth management of the alliance with Shia of Iran on one side and the alliance with the Sunni Islamic groups on the other side. Any negligence or failure to maintain this fragile relation between the Sunni and Shia will be disastrous. -General Abdalla al-Jaili, Popular Defense Force (PDF) General Coordinator.

They espouse a common objective promoting Islamist conspiracies targeting the moderate Muslims that lean in the secular direction, while also encouraging worldwide meetings promoting Islamic orthodoxy. The Sudanese government does not believe all Islamic activity should be under one organization rather it finds strength in the common goal of unifying all Islam. The Bashir government eschews moderate Islam. It has joined Muslim Brotherhood supporter Qatar, Wahhabist Saudi Arabia and Shiite extremist Iran, and balancing relationships.

Throughout this volume we have noted that Mujahideen training has been in Sudan, even before Osama bin Laden was given sanctuary, as laid out in Arab Coalition Plan Appendix B. Under Bin Laden, al Qaeda built a network of training camps for mujahideen in Sudan. Dr. Hassan al-Turabi, mentor of Osama bin Laden, a Western educated King's College London (Law), Sorbonne (PHD) graduate, with both al-Mirghani and the al-Mahdi families, all western educated, have supported the establishment of radical Islam in Sudan since the 1950's. Those training camps spawned trained mujahideen from radical movements around the world funded by Arab businessmen and governments alike. Sheikah Mozah funded mujahideen training in camps and Universities in Sudan in March of 2017, as discussed in Chapter Six of this volume. The training camps, according to the Bashir secret meetings, Oct 11, 2015 were to create a "crusader generation ready to sacrifice for religion and country." These authors discussed the graduation of 24,000 men in various camps around Khartoum in May of 2017. The Bashir regime tells the US they are helping them in the war on terror, while it is actively helping create more global Islamic terror.

Khartoum will not entertain the free democratic non-Sharia Law option of the resistance movements in Sudan. As stated in Bashir's Secret meetings August 31, 2014,

> My personal opinion is that any negotiations with the rebels are a waste of time. They will not get what they want. Also, we don't accept them to return back and stay among us after the assistance they rendered to the enemy to separate the South. Above that, they are still planning to divide and separate the rest of the country. They will continue their business of separation throughout. It is better that we defeat them with military action... - General Imad al-Din Adawy, Chief of Joint Operations

As noted in this volume's Arab Coalition in Plan Appendix B, the Bashir regime's objective is to complete genocidal ethnic cleansing of indigenous African people by 2020, contradicting Lyman's delusional hope that it will "fade away."

It is clear by reading this volume that the whole story is not being presented to the US. Princeton Lyman in his testimony equivocates when confronted by this conundrum saying:

> Nothing is easy when it comes to U.S. policy toward Sudan. So how do we reconcile these factors, i.e., that the government is objectionable in so many of its ways, and that it is nevertheless an important player in a region of great importance to us?

Sudan tactics

Lyman goes on to say that his goal is to give the Sudanese people what they deserve, which he sees as "peace, democracy, and prosperity." However, his definition of these values does not include Islamic Sharia Law, or world domination, that goal Bashir's Generals insist must be included. The authors of this volume have depicted the behavior and rhetoric extolling the ultimate achievement of the Bashir regime's Islamic Revolutionary Vision to become the Caliphate ruling the Sahel region and ultimately the world.

In Chapter Six, the authors have summarized the deceptive tactics used by Bashir's regime. Sudan is a country where the leaders speak sweetly to the diplomats while encouraging people in the street screaming 'Death to America' in Arabic with the express purpose of fooling the diplomats. Lyman's testimony before Congress leaves the US ignoring the cries of millions to 'Stop' the genocide in Sudan.

The problem is multidimensional competing needs with deception. In this situation Sudan is not interested in negotiating anything with the resistance, they are executing a 'killing plan' to implement a vision.

The Generals' in the meetings of 2014, 2015 and 2017 suggest that the US does not know Khartoum as well as Khartoum knows the US. Many of the Generals in these meetings have Western education and use that knowledge about US behavior to plan an effective deception strategy. Khartoum uses patterns of behavior that have been used for centuries by Arab armies and governments.

Lie when needed

The Bashir regime has operated under what Sir Winston Churchill called a "body of lies" in its dealings with the international community, especially with the US. If the lie is to further the cause of the Islamic State or extend the reign of the ruling group, then that is all towards a good end as far as the Bashir regime is concerned. It is the behavior practiced by the Bashir regime reflected in minutes of government strategy meetings. This strategy is used to cover up what they term the Islamic Revolutionary Vision in speeches and media, and then denying anything of the sort was actually said. They also fabricate stories to support their lies, such as calling the resistance 'terrorists.' It has continued to be a very successful tactic for the Sudan government.

Black fight black/enemy fight enemy

'Black fight Black' is a strategy coming from the history of the Prophet Mohammed. He often used two enemies to fight each other rather than using his army to fight. This tactic was used when Bashir hired and trained Riek Machar and his soldiers to destabilize South Sudan, as regime Generals discussed in the meeting in 2014. The Generals also said it was used with Minni Minnawi's forces. This happened both in 2006 signing the Abuja agreement and in 2008 when Adam Salih, commander, signed the extension to Doha agreements. The resistance forces were required to join the Rapid Support Force to fight against any black tribe that refused to join the Government. The other requirement, in both cases, was to integrate these rebel forces by retraining and separating them before dispersing them across various units of the Sudan army to dilute their presence. The strategy is to pit one enemy tribe against another, let them fight it out; then, say it is a reward for the winner to be dispersed into the regime's Revolutionary Force.

From the office to the grave

Co-author, Deborah Martin, has been told often, proverbially, that Bashir's regime puts a plaque behind the new desk chair of people who work for Khartoum, which says, "from the office to the grave," which means we are giving you this office for life, or if you leave this office the result will be the grave. The phrase is used to demoralize the participants in the government illustrating the web of secrecy around government granted positions and the consequences of betraying those confidences.

Buying Time

The Bashir regime uses four ways to buy time.

1. Change the face

Change the face is not just used to describe which mask a person or a country uses, as described earlier in this article, but also is used to describe changing the representative of a country to one more acceptable to the audience, but still espousing the same ideology for the purpose of buying time. It is said that when a new representative is in place, then, it is five more years before anyone figures out that they have been manipulated; and the game is played again. The Vice President of Sudan was Ali Osman Taha during the CPA negotiations. Pressure came from the US and the UN to have some ethnic diversity in the Government, so Taha was replaced with a Darfurian, Alhaj Adam Yusef, who was a Janjaweed leader. The UN and US stopped the pressure even though this official still represented the Islamic State Vision. In Darfur, the Governor of South Darfur was replaced for continuing the atrocities to appease the UN, and was replaced with Abdal Hamid, who has since assisted in removing UN access to Darfur altogether. It was reported that in both cases the people knew these were not the beneficial changes sought by the UN or the US, but these organizations were told they were.

2. Difficult topic first- stall

In negotiations, they will put the most difficult agenda to solve on the table first, then, push the discussion to take a long time and possibly cause the whole event to stall to get their way.

3. Backing off

In battle and in arguments, if they see they cannot win presently, they will choose to back off or even say they are surrendering, so that they can regroup and come back when the enemy least expects it, but more prepared somehow and ready for 'the kill.' This strategy is seen in the history of Prophet Mohammad when he was losing a battle in Medina, he 'backed off' to Mecca, waited some time while he regrouped, then came back with more power to win Medina. Because it is historical, this strategy is used over and over in memory of a great leader. This strategy is seen in how cease fires during the rainy seasons are conducted. When rainy season arrives, the Khartoum government negotiates a cease fire, which lasts conveniently until the rainy season is over. They know their vehicles and planes will be useless for operations during the rainy season. During rainy season, they build their forces and rest their men to be fresh for the battle during the dry or fighting season. The strategy has been effectively used to lull the US and Western observers into believing the Bashir Regime wants peace because he declares this cease fire, when it is a way to ramp up. The 16 cease fires that Khartoum offered in 2016 were followed by resumption of hostilities by the regime, which gave them time to regroup, unnoticed by media, before a new onslaught some days later.

Bashir declaring a cease fire in April of 2016, which he broke shortly thereafter. One of 16 that followed that pattern in 2016. Old patterns die hard.

This strategy was used when the Government declared cease fire in October 10, 2016. Fighting from both sides stopped until the end of November, when an unprovoked attack occurred by government battalions with heavy equipment that had been moved into place during the fire. This attack was also discussed in more detail earlier in this volume in Chapter One.

As we revealed in Chapter Three, the cease fire after sanctions were temporarily lifted by President Obama's Executive Order in January 2017 was broken by Khartoum shortly afterwards with little recognition in the mainstream media.

4. Never implement the terms

Another way to buy time used by the regime is to sign agreements in the presence of international observers and never implement the terms feigning excuses like, "We did our best!!" The Khartoum government regularly agrees to release prisoners as part of an agreement, and then, later comes back and kills them.

In the case of the murder of a USAID employee and his driver in 2008 referenced in this volume, the Bashir government caught the killers and convicted them then announced their escape within days of the conviction. That was likely due to an edict Bashir issued in September of 2007 absolving of guilt in the name of Allah any Mujahideen who killed westerners in Khartoum.

Always fight --cooperation is only to get my way

In the game Prisoner's Dilemma, the truth that cooperation is better than fighting is demonstrated for social psychology classes in the West, even if fighting always produces a win. In the model two-player game both players can win if they cooperate, but if the goal does not include cooperation, then the best option for winning is always fight. Khartoum in its revolutionary tactics has chosen to fight in all cases.

Bashir's Generals in their meetings explain that the Islamic Sudan Republic must win at all costs. The US according to Lyman endeavors negotiating toward an outcome of cooperation, while according to the Generals in 2014, 2015, and 2017, Khartoum's only objective is conquest. Cooperation is seen as only a temporary tool for advancing toward a win. Honor is only given to the winner and trust is virtually nonexistent in the Islamic Revolutionary Vision of the Bashir regime. That is befitting his authority based on the definition of Dar al Islam, or a State ruled by Islam. The win-lose nature of an Islamic political takeover is demonstrated by Khartoum's never-ending goal to cleanse their land of Kufr (the infidels) and the indigenous black African peoples. US government representatives seem to have no understanding of this Islamic doctrine, which prevents them from supporting strong action against such goals and behavior.

Camel in the master's tent

There is a folk tale told in Sudan about a Master who owned a camel that is the underpinning for strategies used by the Khartoum regime. The Master tied his camel outside his tent. One cold night the camel decided he must do something to get warm. So, he put his nose under the edge of the tent, but that was not warm enough. The Master had not noticed and so the camel pushed in until his neck was under the tent. Slowly but surely, the camel pushes in without the Master noticing until the Master is pushed out of the tent door into the cold. The camel had now taken his place inside the warm tent. This is a folk tale illustrating Khartoum's Arab Coalition Plan (see Appendix B) strategy for taking over every village, the country, the Sahel and possibly the world.

The 'Islamo-Arab' Coalition, as Wahid Abdel al-Nour called it in his letter to previous US Special Envoy to Sudan, Donald Booth, in Chapter Two, has been moving into the 'Sudan tent' since the 1881 declaration of Sharia law in Sudan. From the Mahdi of that era until today the Khartoum government especially since the 1950's has been continually pursuing a policy of 'finishing' off the indigenous African resistance committing genocide against indigenous African people. The US may be on the verge of abetting that objective, if it permanently lifts sanctions against the political Islamist regime of President Omar Ahmad Hassan al-Bashir.

Conclusion

As discussed in this volume the Bashir political Islamic regime in Khartoum will never countenance the free democratic non-Sharia Law option that the US espouses. As depicted in this volume the Bashir regime wants nothing to do with the US to promote this parallel universe of rule by secular law.

It uses Islamic cultural strategies and Sharia doctrine and to deceive the US and West in all negotiations.

It conveys in secret documents the completion of genocidal ethnic cleansing of indigenous African peoples by 2020, replacing them with Arab tribes and foreign Islamic Mujahideen including former ISIS fighters.

It pursues an active alliance with Muslim Brotherhood supporter like Qatar, and even extremist Shia Iran seeking the destabilization and overthrow of adjacent African countries in the Sahel region. The objective is to create a Caliphate ruled under Sharia from Khartoum pursuing the Islamic Revolutionary Vision of world domination.

What the people in Sudan deserve is a country free from tyranny and deception. The US was committed after World War II to stop genocide by any means and never let it happen again, especially by pretending it does not exist. Real goals, not laced with deception, are what need to be determined by the US in the case of Sudan. Otherwise, the US may be abetting genocide by Sudan intent on creating a future Caliphate across the Sahel in Africa, a threat to the world.

Chapter Sixteen
Can we stop the Sudan Genocide?

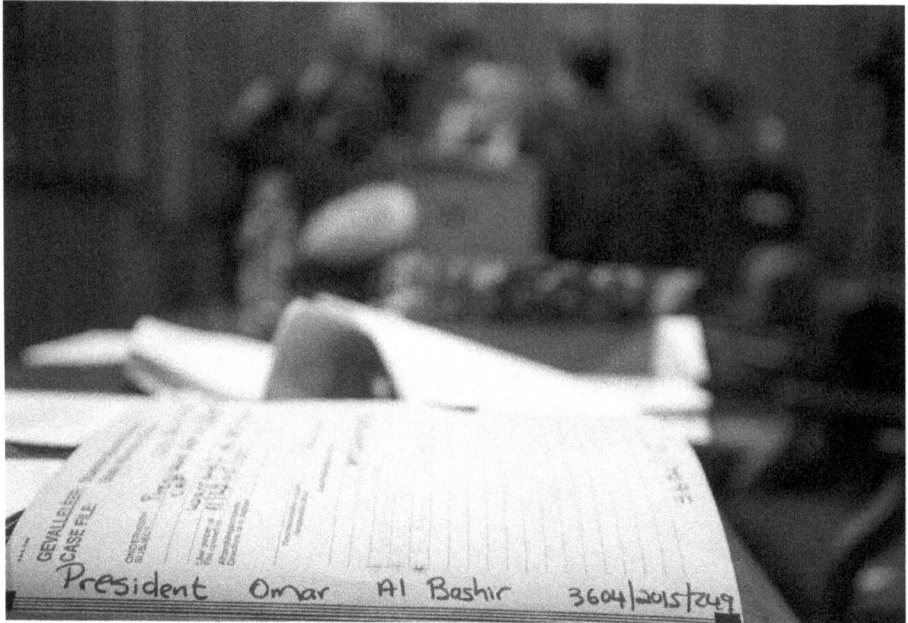

**International Criminal Court Case file against
President Omar Hassan al-Bashir
at hearing of Republic of South Africa High Court 2015
Source: Getty Images**

Background

Spanish essayist, philosopher and poet George Santayana's often cited quote, "those who cannot remember the past are condemned to repeat it," is apt in addressing the conundrum of stopping genocide in Sudan.

That is illustrated by the prescient exchanges between one of the authors of this volume, Lt. Gen Abakar M. Abdallah, and Dr. Sebastian Gorka in both 2010 and 2017.

In 2010, Abdallah had met Gorka at a regional reunion of international graduates of the National Defense University (NDU) in Nairobi, Kenya. At the time, Gorka was a member of the NDU faculty. Abdallah discussed with Gorka how might the population of Darfur be protected against both Bashir regime Janjaweed militia and Lord's Resistance Army terrorists. Gorka suggested the possibility of using 'contractors' to protect vulnerable populations in Internally Displaced Person camps supplanting the ineffective UNAMID protection forces that had been co-opted by the Bashir regime discussed in Chapter Eight. Abdallah told him the ill-

155

trained and equipped UNAMID force was no match for the heavily armed and equipped Janjaweed militias trained by the Khartoum regime to conduct military operations supported by the Sudanese Army and Air Force.

Fast forward to May 2017, when co-author Gordon forwarded a memo to Gorka from Abakar on the deteriorating status in Sudan based on findings discussed throughout this volume. Gorka was then Deputy Assistant to President Trump. Gorka was prompted to respond by recollection of his 2010 discussion with Abakar in Nairobi and indicated to Gordon that he forwarded the memo to presumably the National Security Council.

Notwithstanding Gorka's recent leave-taking from his Presidential aide post, what Abakar concluded in the May 2017 memo frames the basis of recommendations presented in this chapter.

Abakar stated that the conflict in Sudan is not simply one portrayed in the media as involving an internal dispute between two parties, the Bashir regime and resistance movements. Rather, it involves multiple parties; (1) the indigenous African peoples and original citizens of Darfur and the other conflict zones; 2) the replacement Arab settlers that the Bashir regime brought in from foreign countries that comprise the Rapid Support Forces/Janjaweed militia; and 3) the Bashir regime and an Arab cabal that financially supports it, i.e., Saudi Arabia and the emirates of Qatar, Kuwait and the UAE.

The worst of these offenders in the Arab cabal is Qatar. Besides funding, it has supplied weapons and involved Sudan as a Muslim Brotherhood ally seeking to destabilize adjacent governments in Libya, Chad and the Central African Republic. That has materially assisted the Bashir regime in completing its secret Arab Coalition Plan building a 150,000-man jihadist army based on the RSF/Janjaweed militia model seeking to create a Caliphate ruling the Sahel region from Khartoum.

On January 13, 2017, former President Obama issued Executive Order No. 13761 temporarily lifting 20-years of sanctions against the regime of International Criminal Court-indicted President Omar al-Bashir of Sudan. Allegedly, it was because of progress in several tracks, among them human rights, counterintelligence about fugitive Joseph Kony of the Lord's Resistance Army and peaceful settlement of the regime's conflicts with several Sudan resistance groups in Darfur, Nuba Mountains, and the Blue Nile State.

The Presidential order left it to incoming President Trump to respond by July 12, 2017 with a determination about permanently lifting the sanctions. President Trump issued a new Executive order on the evening of July 11th deferring that decision until October 12, 2017. Prior to issuing the new executive order, all 53 members of the US House of Representatives Foreign Affairs Committee sent a letter to President Trump. These Representatives suggested, based on the lack of clear evidence indicating that the five tracks are respected, the sanctions should be maintained. Further, that a new Special Envoy to Sudan and South Sudan be appointed to investigate representations of progress in Sudan. Therefore, any decision should be deferred for at least a year.

The Evidence presented in this book calls for action

The authors of *Genocide in Sudan: Caliphate threatens Africa and the World* has presented a veritable dossier of facts on the ground that constitutes a brief in support of the US House of Representatives Foreign Relations Committee recommendations.

As noted in Chapter 2 by Sudan Liberation Movement [SLM] leader, Abdul Wahid al-Nour, the Bashir regime has calumniously convened national dialogues after signing and ultimately breaking peace accords with Sudanese resistance groups. Following the breakup of such agreements, it has resorted to intensified genocidal ethnic cleansing against indigenous African peoples.

The Bashir regime created a web of deception reflected in secret documents, including a captured Arab Coalition Plan discussed in Chapter Five, to complete genocidal ethnic cleansing of indigenous black African peoples with their replacement by Arab settlers by 2020.

Its duplicity in feigning compliance with the five tracks of Executive Order 13761 was illustrated in the Secret Minutes of the National Political Crisis Committee in Chapter 11. The table talk revealed it had purposely misled the Obama Administration regarding alleged counterintelligence information on the whereabouts of the notorious fugitive Joseph Kony of the Lord's Resistance Army. In fact, a co-author, General Abakar M. Abdallah, had provided that information to USAFRICOM, which did not return acknowledgment.

As illustrated in Chapter 14, the Bashir regime has engaged in a sinister disarmament program feigning recapture of arms from these defenseless indigenous African peoples only to unleash Rapid Support Force/ Janjaweed militias to ethnically cleanse and destroy hundreds of villages, expropriate properties and animal herds, rape women, kill men and forcibly recruit youths into cruel military service.

The Arab Coalition Plan detailed the strategy of replacing the indigenous population with Arabs the regime brings in from foreign countries. The regime's overall strategy is to recruit 150,000 men drawn from Arab tribes and jihadists from across the Sahel region of Africa and Islamic State fighters from the Middle East. The objective is create a new Caliphate ruled under Sharia Supremacism from Khartoum backed by billions of dollars in weapons and grants from across the Arab League. Further, the authors reveal that Qatar and Sudan have engaged in the overthrow of regimes in neighboring Libya, Chad and the Central African

Republic (CAR). The Sudan human toll under Bashir speaks for itself: over 400,000 dead, about 5 million internally displaced and several hundred thousands who have fled to UN refugee camps in Chad, CAR, and elsewhere.

The threat to the US and the world is reflected in efforts by the regime to proselytize its Muslim Brotherhood Salafist Supremacist doctrine abroad. In late January 2017 it was reported that Bashir had deployed a number of Sudanese Sheiks to Mosques in the US. The Qatar Foundation is funding a K-12 Arabic language and culture program in public schools here in America.

The track record of the Bashir Regime in Terms of the UN Convention against Genocide

The United Nations adopted the Convention on the Prevention and Punishment of the Crime of Genocide on December 9, 1948, implemented January 12, 1951. Let us examine Sudan's violations of the Convention's Articles:

Article I
The Contracting Parties confirm that genocide, whether committed in time of peace or in time of war, is a crime under international law which they undertake to prevent and punish.

Article II
In the present Convention, genocide means any of the following acts committed with intent to destroy, in whole or in part, a national, ethnical, racial or religious group, as such:

(a) Killing members of the group; (*to date since 1983, 2.5 million people have died in South Sudan and more than 2 million people have died in the Republic of Sudan.*)
(b) Causing serious bodily or mental harm to members of the group; (*The Sudan government army and policies contributed to those deaths.*)
(c) Deliberately inflicting on the group conditions of life calculated to bring about its physical destruction in whole or in part; (*no food, no water, no medicine, no education, subhuman conditions, poisoned bags of relief food, out of date spoiled medicine, blocked supplies, burning houses and killing animals and driving people into caves.*)
(d) Imposing measures intended to prevent births within the group; (*raping women by Janjaweed as a war strategy.*)
(e) Forcibly transferring children of the group to another group. (*Seizing children and youths as slaves and forcibly impressing them in the army, forcibly taking children from their families.*)

The following acts shall be punishable:
(a) Genocide;
(b) Conspiracy to commit genocide;
(c) Direct and public incitement to commit genocide;

(d) Attempt to commit genocide;
(e) Complicity in genocide.

Article IV
Persons committing genocide or any of the other acts enumerated in article III shall be punished, whether they are constitutionally responsible rulers, public officials or private individuals (President Bashir has been indicted in both 2003 and 2009 for Crimes against humanity by the International Criminal Court at the Hague and evidence revealed in this volume presents that he plans on continuing that behavior.)

Suggested actions.

Herewith are our suggested actions.

- Notwithstanding the announcement by Secretary of State Tillerson, accept the suggestion contained in the June 30, 2017 letter of the US House of Representatives Foreign Relations Committee to appoint an independent minded and qualified Special Envoy to Sudan and South Sudan and supporting team to conduct investigations and prepare a report on conditions in the major conflict zones of Sudan including consultation with Sudan resistance group leaders.
- Defer at least for a year any action resulting in the permanent lifting of sanctions against Sudan pursuant to delivery of the proposed definitive report and its recommendations to the President for his subsequent actions.
- Establish a USAFRICOM 24/7 surveillance program providing real time intelligence on incidents against indigenous African peoples in the threatened conflict zones by the Sudan regime, its military, National Intelligence and Security Service and the Rapid Support Force/Janjaweed militia.
- Establish USAFRICOM liaison with Sudan resistance groups in the conflict zones to provide home guard training for vulnerable internal displaced persons camps in indigenous African conflict zones.
- Establish a USAFRICOM joint intelligence center with allies in the region to monitor Islamist groups and state actors like Qatar and Sudan seeking the overthrow of regimes in the adjacent Northern and Sahel regions of Africa.
- Establish and provision fully operated emergency and acute care health facilities in the conflict zones.

- Create a humanitarian assistance base of operations in an adjacent country with access to the conflict zones for unhampered and tamper proof delivery of food assistance and medicine in drought stricken areas.
- Impose sanctions with established means of redress for Sudan's development and use of prohibited chemical, biological, radiological and nuclear materials.
- Create an international inspection regime for all identified weapons manufacturing facilities in Sudan.
- Sanction both Qatar and Sudan for its support and conduct of insurgent efforts seeking the overthrow of duly constituted governments in the adjacent Sahel region.
- Provide auspices and training for civil society development in Sudan.
- Monitor human rights violations in accordance with US and UN sanctions.
- Consider holding regional or state council elections in Sudan under International Election monitors.

Three former US Administrations – Clinton, Bush II and Obama-have failed to engage in what both former Assistant Secretary of State for African Affairs Susan Rice and Pulitzer Prize winning author of *A Problem from Hell: America and the Age of Genocide,* US UN Ambassador Samantha Power advocated, which was 'robust humanitarian means' to prevent or arrest genocide in Africa, whether in Rwanda or Sudan.

Now, it is the turn of the Trump Administration to address the continuing genocide with the threat of creating a future Salafist Supremacist Caliphate as foretold in 1881 by Mohammed Mahdi and propounded by his progeny down to the current generation in Khartoum. We will soon see if the lessons of history are a guidepost for positive actions. If not grasped, then genocide followed by a new Caliphate may rise threatening the Sahel region of Africa and potentially the world.

Appendix A
Maps of Sudan and Conflict Zones

Sudan

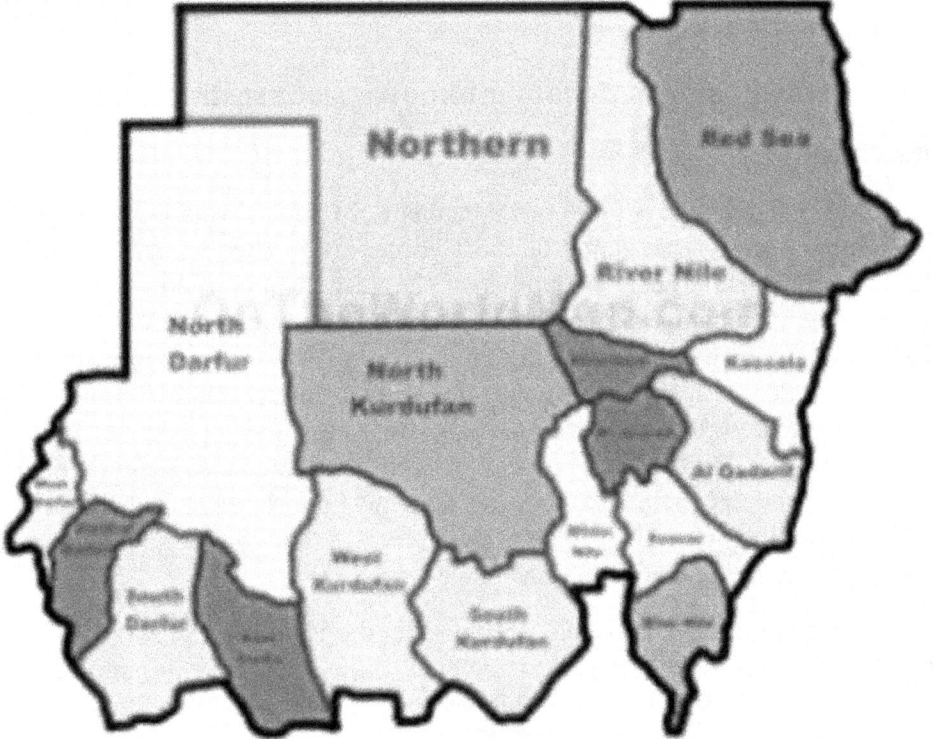

Appendix B
Translation of Arab Coalition Secret Plan

There are comments in brackets by the authors of this book.

Date Translated: 16/05/2015

Arab Coalition document known as Guresh 1 and 2

Description

The Arabic Language version of this document of 11 pages was captured during the fighting between the Rapid Support Forces (RSF) (Reorganized Janjaweed Militias) and Darfur rebels in October of the year 2014 in Donky Hush, North Darfur. The document was found in an abandoned military track belonging to the RSF. The document is containing different Guresh statements or evaluations of the Arab Coalition project that began in 1987 and continuous until the last evaluation in 2014. Their objective was and still to eradicate the people of Darfur and occupy the land. I have tried and translated the document in English Language so that the people particularly for English Language readers to understand the intention of the Arab Janjaweed and the Arab Coalition in cooperation with the regime in Khartoum.

The most important part of this document is the evaluation of 2014 in which they distributed the entirely Darfur region to different Arab tribes and they are intended to finish their project in the near future. If the Arab Coalition plan left unchecked, then Janjaweed militias will committee more genocide atrocities in Darfur.

I kept the original documents of the Arabic Language version. In case anyone wanted to use for reference; I will send it to him, as he required. I also made some comments in Brackets and placed them in Italics. My comments are just to clarify some points.

The phrases with Italics are my comments and are not part of the translation or the document.

Statement Declaring Creation of Arab Coalition *[The first Arab Coalition document was issued in 1987)*

The essential document declaring the creation of the Arab Assembly against Darfur was issued in Mars 1987. It was renewed followed the evaluation of its advantages and disadvantages of the past period as well as the objectives that had been achieved since 1992. After 11 years, the implementation of the document was renewed in 2003. However, the job had not been completely finished due to several obstacles emerged during this period. These obstacles include internal problems occurring between the Arab tribes, lack of adequate resources, the starting of rebellion in Darfur region from non-Arab tribes, and the support of the international community to Darfur cause. Sudan is also being placed in the list of states sponsoring of terrorism and the accusation directed against some government authorities by the International Criminal Court; of committing war crimes, crimes against humanity, and genocide in Darfur. On top of these authorities is President Omer Bashir himself. Others include Musa Hilal, Ahmed Haroun, and Ali Kosheeb

There are also several other problems that made this project not to be realized. Some members thought of personal interests and diverted the funds collected for the purpose of executing this plan to personal benefits. There are also problems of some tribes who were initially agreed to support the project but they withdrew when they perceived that this project is not for their interest in the long future. They were executing plans that at the end will destroy them. The list below is some of the tribes who withdrew their support to the project:

Bani Hissein -------Maalia ------- Birgid-------Tama------- Berti

Ghimir------Dorock------Habania-------Saada------Dajo

There is also flow of immigrants of some tribes come from neighboring states due to some internal conflict occurring in their countries. These countries include Chad, Niger, Mali, and Central African Republic.

The Executive Committee must move and make general review of these objectives and develop new plans suitable with the present situation. Whenever we face obstacles or problems in our way, we must go back consult with the sources that are in charge of making plans. They can make necessary adjustments or modify plans in order to remove obstacles that blocking the continuation of the work. The separation of South Sudan also brought challenges

166

that disrupted the execution of this program. It caused security instability in the areas of Missiyria and Dinka alike.

Document No-1

The Arab race that known today as Arab tribes in Darfur entered Sudan in 15th century AD. Despite their division into various groups, in reality they belong to one origin.

These tribes settled in two areas of the Darfur region: One group settled in South Darfur state in which the Arabs occupy 80% of the region's land space. *[Arabs have only the areas of De'ean, Buram, Ida al Khanem, and Rhihedal Birdi. These areas represent less than the half of the regions land space and Arabs are minority even in these areas...Abakar].* The second group settled in North Darfur region in which they occupy the larger part of the north, center, east, and west. The Arab tribes occupy 55% of the state's land space *[...there are no Arabs in North Darfur region accept the family of Musa Hilal that has a village known as Mesteria and Zeiyadiya also has one village named Koma...Abakar].* The Arabs are representing more than 70% of Darfur's population [*...Arabs may represent only15% or 20% of Darfur's population*...Abakan]. Throughout the centuries, the Arab tribes in Darfur played an important role in the formation of the region's identity. The Arabs in this part of our country are the makers of the civilization that constitutes the true existence of this region in the areas of governance, religion, and language *[...Tenure are the people that brought Islam religion in Darfur and established Islamic kingdoms in in 12th century AD in the areas of Ain Frah and Ain Siro, North Darfur. They built Mosques that the remnants of their structures are still standing. Dr. Shogar Ahmed Mohamed Hamid mentioned in his book." Aduwa Tunjur" that Sultan Shaw Dorsheet of Tunjur ruled by Islamic Sharia and Tunjur were the people who brought Islam in Darfur and ruled by Islamic Sharia and not Arabs they are nomadic people and have no any background of Koran or Islamic education from the ancient days to this date. They engaged in animal husbandry...Abakar].* Arabs have played an important role in constituting of the present Sudan. They were the main sources of defense and fought for al Mahdi Revolution. Sacrificed and died in defending this country. Over the centuries, they contributed in political stability, economic development, civilization, and cultural advancement in Darfur in particular and Sudan in general. By this, we confirmed and will confirm that we preserved and will preserve the unity of this country and protect its territorial integrity.

Mr. Prime Minister *[...this message was addressed to prime Minister Sadiq al Mhadi in 1987 and he or his government had approved the request and provided limited financial and arms to some Arabs of Darfur in the name of popular defense and they attacked Fur tribes burned their villages and cut down fruit plantations in 1987. Followed the coup of 1989 that overthrown al Mahdi's government and brought the National Islamic Front under the leadership of the current President Omer Hassan al-Bashir to power that continued the same to some Darfur Arabs. Presidents Gaddafi and Bashir made joint cooperation and provided weapons, logistics, and*

167

financial support to Arabs in Wadi Saleh. This was the reason that brought Osama bn Laden to wadi Saleh, Central Darfur Region in 1993 and opened training camps for Janjaweed Militias.... Abakar]

Those who study the government systems in the world defined the regional government in several ways. It is generally means decentralization in which the power will be delegated to the people of the region for the purpose of making good political, administrative, and economic policies. By all means, the governance of the Darfur region should be given to the sons of the Arabs of the region who should be representing leadership and power that be shared according to their tribal divisions; so that they can participate in decision making process. We become majority without weighs and leaders without people:

We representing 70% of the region's population *[.... they may represent 15% to 20%.... Abakar]*

The educated Arabs, representing more than 40% of the educated elite of the region in which hundreds among them have university degrees, and tenth of them have Master and PHDs, specialized in different areas *[.... Arabs are minority and they are the less educated people in Darfur because most of their children are used to keep animals, therefore, they cannot represent 40%...Abakar]*

Participating in national income not less than 15% at federal level *[...false. They raise only animals...Abakar]*

Participating in more than 90% of the income of the region *[not true, they have only few livestock, no farming and trade. All Darfur people raise animals make trade, and farming... Abakar]*

Participating more in military and security forces and sacrificing in the defend of the country

On political side, we are offering 14 members of the national assembly representing Arabs and participating by 18 members in the general Assembly

Mr. President

What we declared is the truth and it ensures that these tribes have an important political, social, and economic weighs in this region. So we request at less have of the political positions in the regional government to be given to Arabs and we should representing the region in the central government. We suspect that the negligence of the Arabs and not allowing them to participate in government could lead to slip problem and fall into the hands of ignorant and an unexpected disaster could occur. The injustice from the near is more severe to oneself, in realty.

In conclusion, we assure all the Sudanese citizens that we are not calling for separation and split but requesting our rights and equality and to live in united Sudan under the banner of freedom and democracy.

The Members of the Committee delegated from the Arab Assembly

[...Founders of the Arab Coalition and the masterminds of Janjaweed Militias ...Abakar]:

Mr. Abdullah Massar

Mr. Charef Ali Jaafar

Mr. Ibrahim Yacoub

Mr. Hussein Hassan Basha

Cheief Hamid Biyutu

Mr. Taj Adin Ahmed al Hilo

Mr. Ayoub Bolola

Mr. Mohamed Kof Alshataly

Mr. Mohamed Zakria Daldom

Mr. Alhadi issa Dabaka

.Mr. Ateib Abu Shama

Mr. Sandaka Daowd

Mr. Haroun Ali Sunusi

Mr. Omer Abdeljabar

Mr. Abdallah Yahaya

Mr. Suleiman Jabir Abakar

Chief Mohamed Yacoub al Umda

Mr. hamid Mohamed Kherallah

Mr. Mohamed Aduma Omer

Mr. Abderhaman Ali Abdenabi

Mr. Ahmed Shata Ahmed

Mr. Abubakar Abo Alamin

Mr. Jabir Ahmed al Rheh

We had learned in Guresh-1 the birth of new Guresh and some programs, but the developments that the country is witnessing and new political events with its internal and external dimensions required us to take a pause and make reflection to recall the objectives, make reviews of the plans and consolidate the achievements for the purpose of attaining your noble objectives.

You know Ja'alyyin, Danagla, and Shaigiya ruled us for about a century. However, they pretend to be Arabs, they are part and parcel of the Nubian race and this group will remain cliquing in power in the country forever. The three groups recently sworn that power should be circulated only among them.

Guresh is passing through difficult times. What required from all of us especially the two partners (the Arab of Kordofan and Darfur) to forgive one another and leaves ideologies and sectarian divisions for the purpose of achieving our noble objectives and consolidates what we had already achieved. It is necessary to work to attain the objectives through respecting of the following principles:

1. The latest time is 2020
2. The objective is Guresh-2 (to control Darfur)
3. The temporary objective- the 6 Darfur States
4. The plans, programs, and resources

This will be in two levels: -

1. **Internal:**
2. Take care of education both vertical and horizontal and produce cadres specialized in different areas (political, economic, media, security, and military)
3. Establish economic generating institutions
4. Enter into military and security organizations
5. Continue to pretend in order to maintain cooperation with the present government
6. Retention of the existing work relationship with key personalities who belong to the ruling tripartite coalition (Danagla, Shaigiya, and Ja'alyyin) in the government
7. Know the importance of tribes live in border regions and inform the government to give more support, arming, and training of (popular defense forces, Mujahcdeen, and forces of peace)
8. Inform all trained from relatives to join peace forces
9. Keep relationship and good understanding with Dinka
10. Fully respect the points of Shaheen operation of the South Kordofan

11. Resolve the problem between Nuhood and Fullah and encourage relatives in the country to stop the internal conflicts that exhausting our strength
12. Do not raise the issue of petroleum oil prior to extraction
13. Stop rumors about Nyala incident and try to release the Fursan
14. Secure all grazing areas in Sudan, Chad, and Central African Republic
15. Fight the idea of landownership that existed (Hawakir, Diyar) by all means
16. Show our national effort against the non-Arab tribes in West Sudan as national against the extension to the rebellion in Darfur
17. Widen the gap of loss of confidence between the government in Khartoum and black tribes by pushing their leaders to behave in more extremism ways by expressing of injustice segregations occurred in West (Darfur)
18. Try to obtain more executive positions in the regional and central government
19. Preserve the achievements and programs of Jamous of Western Darfur and accepting its consequences
20. For Traifi 2 and traifi 3 to continue work to allow the 2 Gureshes to succeed in Darfur (eradicate the entire population and fully occupy Darfur)
21. Prepare for any elections coming in the 6 Darfur states
22. Keep secret, discipline, and do not talk or mention of anything of the country of Bagara
23. It's necessary to take care and direct positive press
24. Its necessary to improve financial status of Guresh
25. It's necessary to develop members of Mali in Guresh
26. 3 of the senior authorities of Guresh must remain in the National Congress Party and carry out decisions according to solutions

External:

1. Strengthen coordination and consultation with members of Guresh (Arabs) in neighboring countries
2. Develop strategic understanding similar to the one of Baghalani, Acyl, and Cheick Ibn Omer with Libya *[...Three were from Chadian Arabs and they were rebel leaders that Gaddafi provided them with financial and military support to overthrow governments of the republic of Chad in 1998s]*
3. Develop programs of racing of horses and camels to benefit and fostering relationship with our Arab brothers in the Middle East states

Arab Coalition or Arab Assembly

To those members who sworn under the oath of the leadership of the Arab Assembly have to carry out extensive meetings for the purpose of executing conditions agreed upon by the Executive Committee and their leaders. First, hold meetings with all tribes who live near those areas that their owners are expelled by force and burned down their villages. The traditional chiefs and sheiks have to be responsible for their followers so as to complete this task with confidence. Second, make general meetings for all the Arab and non-Arab tribes as well as volunteers from other tribes and use them. Tribes such as Zagawa could be used in war purposes such as military training, and guides (showing them roads and areas they do not know). Be carefully so that they should not perceive that these actions in the future would remove them from their land. Below are all the points that should be executed:

1. Seize all livestock and resources from Fur tribe
2. Kill their representatives, leaders, educated, and confine the rest of them in big cities, prisons, and kill them whenever there is a chance.
3. Keep all government resources that can assist people on making complaints, or can be used in emergence cases, transportation, or communication so that they could not communicate between one another
4. Place camps of Arab fighters (Janjaweed) on high mountains so that the attackers cannot approach them
5. Attacking areas that have strong resistance with large forces
6. Deploy new arrivals from Chad, Groups of Idriss Jamous, and Hissein Habre to the areas of western Darfur region as followings:

   a) Wadi Salih

   b) Mockjar

   c) Wadi Kaja

7. Deploy the popular defense forces that came from Kordofan in the following areas:

   a) Jebel Marra b) South and South of Jebel Marra, and Kas

   b) South and South of Jebel Marra, and Kas

   c) Wadi Barai

All who sworn have to be responsible and keep all points mentioned in order to achieve the victory? Know that the enemy forces constitutes from the infidels and heresies. For this reason, deploy our forces according to the way suit the area.

The Arab Assembly Committee of the Region

Branch in Charge of war operation

Date: 1992 DA

Document No-4

Political Committee Coordinating Council

Report of the mission of the committee mentioned above to the localities.

The committee moved on Monday 10/11/2003 at 5 O'clock in the evening to Buram local district and arrived in the same night at 10 O'clock. The committee began its work immediately at arrival with the traditional leaders, local chiefs, and executives (senior government officials in the district), and elders.

Followed the explanation of the purpose their visit they opened question and answer session to allow the audiences to comment, ask questions, bring ideas, or propositions. The audiences expressed their happiness and welcomed all the ideas that came from the committee despite the fact that it came late. They replied all the questions and the importance of these clarifications for the audiences are:

1- This idea has to continue until suitable results are achieved
2- Consult those who have knowledgeable, experiences, ideas, and economy
3- Ensure fair distribution of positions and wealth especially at the regional and national levels
4- Try quickly to reduce tensions between the Arab tribes
5- Consider the problem in the point of religious view and explain in Islamic terms
6- Spread this idea to all the Sudan
7- Change the name of Darfur into a suitable one
8- It is necessary to use press, documenting, and make research

Followed the advises, brother Omer Ali al Khaly the Khalifa of Nazir (Traditional Chief) was appointed to be the coordinator of the Arab Assembly in Buram locality to coordinate with the people.

Second, appointed the secretary of National Congress Party in the locality to take the signatories of all the members of the Buram council and send the list immediately to Nyala.

At the end of the meeting, all who were present made their oath to work side by side for unification and make this idea to succeed. The second day, the committee visited Nazir (Sultant) Salah Ali al Khaly and explained to him the idea. He welcomed the idea and then the committee visited the Presidential Commissioner in his residence and he also welcomed the idea with absoluteness.

The committee visited the representative of the local district (which is also the headquarters of the local Assembly). He completely supported the project and requested from the National Congress Party Secretary to take signatories and provide transportation to carry the members of the council at any time they wanted to move.

On 11/11/2003 the committee visited Nazir of Tulus Fulata (Traditional Chief) and held a meeting with local chiefs, politicians, government officials. The representative of traditional chief thanked the coordinating Assembly representing the visiting committee; and pointed out the seriousness of the present situation the necessity of unification required to execute this project. He also introduced members of the committee with the audience and offered to exchange talks. All the members agreed on the following:

1- All agreed that it is necessary to unite and execute
2- Organize media committee
3- Ensure the continuity of the presence of our brothers from the republic of Chad
4- Spread the ideas among university students
5- Open roads and seasonal resting places for herders
6- Unify, organize, and work to execute policy
7- Create good relationship with central government
8- Create an organ to exchange security plans and intelligence with the government
9- Create suitable economy plans to ensure security
10- Develop and use the traditional chiefs
11- Issue a clear Memorandum of the Arab Assembly
12- Keep secret

Elected county Chief Yusuf Omer Khatir as coordinator of the local Assembly of Tulus and appointed the secretary of the National Congress Party to take signatories of the members of the council and send the list immediately to Nyala.

It was requested that the representative of Tulus provide transport for the members of the council whenever they required.

Then the committee met with County Chief Ahmed Sammani al-Bashir who ensured his support of the project and gave the following advises:

1- Required from all Arab leaders to propose the idea of unity and maintain the execution
2- Inform the County Chief Madibo of Rezeigat to take this job seriously with all leaders in the areas

On 12/11/2003 the committee visited the locality of Rehid al Birdi and met with the tribal chiefs and political leaders.

They collectively supported the idea and ensured their desired to work to succeed and issue. They issued the following advices:

1- Declare public unity since this representing an important project
2- Keep information secret especially regarding the internal plans
3- Make a clear call for unity
4- Select the objectives and work to execute
5- Move from defensive to offensive positions and take initiatives to avoid roamers and lies that destroy the society
6- Study events carefully to ensure their success
7- Be open minded in dealing with others
8- Remove the popular defense forces and police from Darfur because they have committed a number of offenses
9- Create an economic plan to support the project
10- Remove completely the government of South Darfur by using absolute Mechanical majority
11- Change the name of Darfur by another suitable name
12- Revise the civil service with Khartoum government
13- Encourage the sons of Arab tribes to enter into military, police, and security forces

After the oath, Brother Yusuf Mohamed Yusuf was elected as coordinator of the locality. The Secretary of the National Congress Party was also elected.

For the information, all the Arab tribes were represented in the meeting especially the Salamat tribe that settled in Rehed al Birdi.

On Thursday 13/11/2003 the committee held meetings with local chiefs and politicians in Ida al Fursan. After the explanation of the purpose of the visit, the committee listened to the ideas presented by the audiences and carried out the following decisions:

1- Employ the university graduates of Arab origin in the government institutions
2- Safeguard the foundation of the project and develop it
3- By all means provide protection to politicians from Arab tribes who are responsible of this project
4- Change the original names of the places in Darfur to better ones
5- Strengthen social cohesion of the Arab tribes and organize to exchange visits among each other
6- Establish clear economic bases
7- Publish works and achievements of the Arabs in press without hesitation
8- Organize Janjaweed to work as benevolent and protect the Arab tribes
9- Fully respect the Arab leaders especially the committee of the council
10- Mediate to resolve problems in the state between all the tribes to achieve confidence and gain the respect of others
11- Take care of external problems especially trade across the borders
12- Keep information secret
13- Benefit from university graduates and results of scientific researches
14- Enhance the administrative and executive organs in the South Darfur capital
15- Revise the plans that were made in Goz Dongo area and water project that was approved in the name of Fursan
16- Revise the immigration to Nyala

The executive committee of the Arab Assembly met to evaluate the activities of the members in all areas and study and clarify some of the appointments of the ministers of black origin in the regional governments and ensure to continue the struggle and unity in this difficult period. This project cannot be executed without strong men.

The Higher Committee of the Arab Assembly carried out the following decisions:

1- Create difficulties on the way of the regional governments and use all resources available so as not to be able to execute their policies and programs of development
2- Do everything possible to disrupt government services in the areas occupied by non-Arab tribes in order to make them feel the weakness of the government and its failure to provide necessary means for life
3- Increase the volunteers in areas occupied by non-Arab tribes to create insecurity problems and stop production and kill their leaders
4- Create disputes between non-Arab tribes so as not to be united
5- The members of the Assembly occupying senior positions have to do the following:

a) Concentrate on providing services on the areas of the Arab Assembly

b) Do not employ non-Arabs in important positions and try to create obstacles for those who occupy positions and work in administration. Whenever there is chance, kill them

c) Try by all means to create instability in schools in non-Arab populated areas

Support No-1

Objectives that had been Achieves

Followed the revision of the strategic objectives and temporary plans that had been executed, the executive committee found that there is an estimated of 60% from the total plans had been achieves; followed the divisions of Darfur states into five parts and areas.

The remained 40% as follows:

1-   The areas remained in North Darfur state

a)   All Areas east of Darfur accept the Zaiyadia land

b)   Areas of Dar Zagawa accept Gouba and its surroundings

c)   Areas of Ain Siro because of the presence of armed rebels of Abdel Wahid

d)   A strip along the Eastern Jebel Marra and North of South Darfur state

e)   Only small portion of the region's population remained outside the big cities and Internally Displaced camps however, this could be finished at any time

f)   80% of the schools are closed down

g)   Geographically, the area had been changed according to the plan

2-   Central Darfur state

There is a good relationship between the government and some of the leaders in the Central Darfur State. The Assembly should select them and draw benefit and use them to kill the tribal leaders, youth, and activities prior to finishing period because they can disrupt the execution of this project.

The other areas that left are small and occupied by rebel movement lead by Abdel Wahid in Jebel Marra but we controlled all the roads leading to the regional headquarters of Zalingui

The area of the Western Darfur State remained:

a)   The Headquarters of the State (Geneina) and the areas in the North of the state

b)   All the villages in the state had been completely burned down

c)   All the locales had left the villages and entered into the main cities and Internally Displaced camps

d)   Fully controlled the politics and security of the state

Supplementary Document No-2

The future plans that needed to be executed

Up to this year 2014, it remained only six (6) years from the date given to the Arab Assembly to finish its project. The latest time is 2020. We have not been able to execute this project according to the plan because there are large spaces still not under our control.

As a result, the Executive Committee divided the rest of the areas of the Darfur region to those new comers to settle in it and work fast as this period required finishing the project:

1- North Darfur state

a)   Areas Northeast of the state

b)   Dar Berti- We must support and reinforce Zeyadiya to occupy this area. Berti and Zeyadia are the two important parts to execute the objective of the Arab Assembly

c)   The Southeast of the State- the Rezeigat must extend to north up to the locality of Laiit Jaranebi and its surroundings and settle the Rezeigat that coming from Chad. It's necessary to work in these areas in order to fully control

d)   The Headquarters of the state- The present governor must be removed. Try by election or any other means to take the position of the governor

e)   Areas of Dar Midob extended to the areas of Northeast of Kordofan state to be handed over to those who will come from Niger and Mali through the assistance of Rerelgat and Zeyadiya

f)   Areas South Southeast of the state in addition to Eastern Jebel Marra extended up to Saga-Anaam- Dar al Salam- and extended up to Dar Marareit should be handed over to Arab tribes of Hamdania and Ireigat

g)   Areas of Shanguel Toubaye and areas of the Eastern Jebel Marra should be handed over to Arab tribes of Aulad Mansur, Maharia, and Um al Khora

h)   Areas of Dar Zagawa divided as follows:

i)   Areas of Um Sidir, Jira, Anka, Bredick, Bere, and Donki Hush should be handed over to Arab tribes of Missiyria and Zeyadiya

j)   Areas of Abdel Shakur, Disa, Bir Maza, Jineck, Wakhaem, and some parts of Wadi Hawar should be handed over to Arab tribe of Maharia coming from Chad

k)   Areas of Abu Delegue, Khazan Orchi, Um Baru, and Gerer should be handed over to Arabs of Jalul and Mahamid

l)   Areas of Abu Gamra, Abu Jidat, Adar, and Ida al Kher should be handed over to Arab tribes of Ireigat, Wisegat, and new comers

m)   Areas of Kornei, Furawiya, Bu ba, and Tine should be annexed to the Republic of Chad according to the agreement with the present government

2- South Darfur State-

a) Dar Birgid, the northern strip including the following areas:

-Nyanjo Bro, Nyanjo commondo, Duma, Adua, Juruf, Hamara, Salwa, Jimeza Korteiga, Amly Sakit, Malul, Shawiya, Amar Jadeed, Merching Locality, and Abu Hamra should be handed over to Arab Aulad Mansur the new arrivals under the leadership Mohamed Hamdan Hemeti {Mohamed Hamadan Hemeti is the Commander of the RSF. He is originally immigrated from Arada, Chad in 1995...Abakar).

b) Areas East of Nyala: Including the areas of Khazan Jadeed, Sheria, Mahajiria, Sido, Yasin, Silia, Kahsib, Sani Afando, and Am Kherat should be handed over to Rezeigat coming from Central African Republic

c) The areas of Khor Abeche, al Kalaka, Jufara, Nigaiya, and Kurunje should be handed over to the new comers of Misseriya

d) Areas of Dar Dajo- Bilail, Amkardus, Amgunya, Hijer, Marla, Am Zilegha, Karmal, Abu Azam, Fasha, Undur, Taasha, and Kilo 28 should be handed over to Rizeigat Etefat

e) Locality of Gereda Um dul and its surroundings should be handed over to the Arab Maharia coming from the Central African Republic

g) The Locality of Kateela, Am Takena should be handed over to Arab Bani Halba in addition to new comers from Chad

h) Dar Maalia should be handed over to Rizeigat coming from Mali.

Signatures of the Traditional Chiefs of Arab *Tribes [These are the Arab traditional chiefs who accepted the call of Arab Coalition and mobilized the Janjaweed that committed genocide, war crimes, and the crimes against humanity..Abakar]*

Name	Tribe	Area
Nazer Alhadi Issa Dabaka	Bani Halba	Seraif
Nazer Ismael Adam Hamid	Bani Hissein	Seraif
Nazer al Tijani Abdel Ghadir	Misseriya	Niteaga
Umda Mohamed Yacoub Ibrahim	Chief of Tarjam	Mosko
Umda al-Bashir Musa Abdel Malik	Chief of Salamat	Rihedal Birdi
Umda Ibrahim Abdallah Jadallah	Eteifat	Um Siyali
Umda Ali Zakin	Bani Halba	Markondi
Umda Mohamed Habeeb	Bani Halba	al Saragh
Umda Abdallah Adam Idriss	Salamat	Kutum
Umda Mohamed Suleiman	Bani Halba	Kutum
Umda Mohamed Ahmed Abdelrahim	Mahadi	Kutum
Umda Sinin Alshari	Bani Halba	Idal Khanam
Umda Hassan Mohamed	Bani Halba	Idal Khanam
Umda Mohamed Ahmed Mocktar Manzul	Bani Halba	Kalan Kora
Umda Hilal Adam Ibrahim	Bani Halba	Idal Khanam
Umda Cheick Adin al Naem	Bani Halba	Idal Khanam
Umda Adamou Bakhit Situr	Tunjur	Rural area of Kas
Umda Aduma Adam Hissein	Taalba	Rural area of Kas
Umda Tajadin Abdallah Jibril	Ireigat	Kutum
Umda Adam Sockoyu	Saada	Mulam
Umda Anor Akola Khalid	Misseriya	Nomad
Umda al khaly Adam Jadeed	Misseriya	Wadi Salih
Umda Aliyan Breema Tonbo	Hawat	Kas
Umda al Nor al kher Hamdan	Misseriya	Um Dukun

Abderahaman Abdallah Maltur	Tarjam	Nyala, Bilail
al Sheik Mohamadeen Adud Mhadi	Maharia	Kutum
al Sheik Musa Hilal Abdallah	Mahamid	Kutum
al Sheik Abdallah Hamid al Nor	Sheik of herders	Rural area of Kas
al Sheik Mohamadeen Ibrahim Hamad	Mahadi	Rural area of Kas
al Sheik Abdallah Dausa	Tarjam	Nyala
al Sheik Kabir Abdallah Hassaballah	Maamda	Mulam
al Sheik Omer abdai Mohamed	Rizeigi, Mahamudi	Wadi Salih
al Sheik Osman Mohamed maki	al zibelat	Kabkabiya
al Sheik Adamou Adudu Breema	Rizeigat	Wadi Salih
al Sheik Sakin Ismael Mohamed	Salamat	Wadi Salih
al Sheik Osman Abubakar Abderahim	Rizeigat Mahamudi	Wadi Salih
al Sheik Daowd Abdallah Jaranebi	Tarjam	Nyala Timbisko
al Sheik Hamid Jaranebi Idriss	Maharia	Kutum
al Sheik Mohamed Ishack Omer	Maarba	Kas
al Sheik Fuwad Ali al Nur	Naweiba	Nyerteti, Jebel Marra
al Sheik Joda Afandi yusuf	Mhamudi	Zalingui
al Sheik Abdallah Adam Ahmed	Massaleit	Kas

Appendix C
Translation of Minutes of Sudan Political Crisis Committee, June 18, 2017

The crisis that occurred between Qatar on one side and Saudi Arabia, United Arab Emirate, Bahrain and Egypt come as the result of disagreements between the two parts: The first part is combating of terrorism which Saudi Arabia, United Arab Emirate, Bahrain and Egypt are supported. The second part is the supporting and financing of terrorism in which Qatar is unjustly fully accused of supporting and hosting of terrorists. Qatar has been supporting and hosting those people that had been unjustly fully forced out of their countries.

As an Islamic movement, we have strong relationship with Muslim Brothers and Hamas leadership because we are originally come from Muslim Brotherhood organization. We have a strong attachment with Muslim brothers because they supported us to maintain our Islamic government in Sudan. Through their support, we have been able to overcome many regional and international conspiracies. What is happening to Qatar is the action of targeting Muslim Brothers and Islamic organizations in the world?

The problem began with the visit of Trump to Saudi Arabia who organized a conference for the leaders of Muslim countries for US President to brief them. The conference that we have been invited to attend but Saudi Arabia requested an excuse by saying that the Americans refused that my name to be included. I was expecting King Salman to cancel the conference since the Americans refused my presence as I am considered an ally participating by military forces defending Saudi Arabia. Now, we recognized where our position is. The conference and its results do not bother us.

 The conspiracy against Qatar and Muslim Brothers occurred through conspiracy of Abdel Fatah al Sisi, Saudis and Emirates to eliminate Muslim Brothers. It is known the enemy of Emirate leaders is The Muslim Brothers. Abdel Fatah al Sisi fears Muslim Brothers can threaten his government similar to Emirate, Bahrain and Saudi Arabia in the extension of the Islamic movements seeking to establish government in the Kingdom. There is a dispute between Muslim Brothers and Abdel Fatah al Sisis and Emirates because the latter two support Khalifa Hafter to become president of Libya. This move will threaten our government in Sudan and will end our interest and place our Muslim Brothers in danger.

We financed the Islamic movements, ended Gaddafi's government, assisted Morsi's election campaign and enabled Muslim Brothers to come to power in Egypt. All these activities we realized through the help of Qatar and Iran. Saudi Arabia needs us to determine our position in relations to Gulf crisis. Are we going to clearly declare our support to Qatar because it has been assisting and supporting us in many different fields especially during difficult moments? There are some members of the Muslim Brothers who frankly called us to stand with Qatar in its crisis. Or do we support the Saudi Arabian position? Because of it, we have cut our relations with Iran and are participating in Saudi-led military campaign defending Saudi Arabia. We recognize the big role Saudi Arabia played in the partial lifting of sanctions imposed on us by the US who promised to lift all the sanctions on July 12 through Saudi Arabia. Or do we support in the mediation initiated by Kuwait between the two parts for the sake of finding a complete and fast solution to remove Qatar from its crisis with small losses and make Muslim Brothers to avoid confrontations? I will go to Saudi Arabia tomorrow and meet with King Salman and explain to him our position. Saudis want us to cut our relations with Qatar, but this cannot be possible. Our position goes with our interest.

The Situation inside SPLM-N comes with developments that brought Hilu to confrontation following his long period of absence that made his decisions seem unimportant inside the SPLM-N. Hilu came up with two new requirements, which are self-determination and maintaining SPLA-N army. These ideas, we reject. We will not negotiate with Hilu and some of the Nuba commanders. These are sons of the Nuba Mountains who support him to become the leadership of SPLM-N and should not be allowed to continue. They must be weakened, targeted and dismantled or we will carry out a diplomatic campaign at regional and international level to isolate their group politically. We will not accept a peace deal or negotiations with Hilu. We support Malik Agar's legitimacy and his group through the use of government institutions and the African Union (AU) to achieve this objective. If sanctions are lifted the defeat of Hilu is easy.

HIlu and some sons of Nuba who are rebels have a destructive project. They want to divide Sudan to execute South Sudan plan, but we will not allow this to happen.

We support the movement of Agar and Yasir Arman through diplomatic and media coverage in the internal and external to absorb the shock caused by Hilu and use the crisis to benefit Agar because he has taken a strategy of calming the situation and preventing the escalation and they remained in a position of a victim and self-defense. They also emerged as the part maintaining the position of cooperation and positive approach with the government to find a solution acceptable to end the crisis. The information possessed by the Agar and Arman group is important to defeat Hilu. Our war with Hilu and his supporters and SPLA-N will be intelligence and security to disrupt internallly and create political, military and tribal problems.

Lifting of economic sanctions and removal of Sudan from the list of 'states supporting of terrorism' does not mean that we cut our relations with the

Muslim Brotherhood organization and other Islamic movements or expel its leaders from Sudan. There are no guarantees to international politics especially when the US President is facing legal problems in America. The Islamic movement is targeted by campaigns against its interests and existences in all the world countries and its connection to the terrorism has distorted its efforts of achieving stability. The reasons behind this are known because of our efforts in South Sudan, Libya, Central African Republic (CAR) and Somalia.

We reject accusations against us of supporting terrorism despite our continuous efforts with our brothers and participation in the Islamic alliance of combating terrorism. As a result, no one has the right to accuse us of terrorism because they chose Muslim Brothers for political objectives and for the interest of Egypt, Sisi and Hafter. Our support will go to our brothers in Egypt and Libya to continue struggle until we are totally in control of the Libyan land.

Sudan succeeded to build strong relations with Saudi Arabia, which is the gateway to US and Israel. We use Saudi Arabia and Emirate to lift US sanctions and then declare our position in relation to the Gulf crisis. We cannot continue in the alliances with the presence of Sisi of Egypt. If sanctions are lifted, it is our right to reestablish relations with Iran because it is a regional force, which represents Islam, and it cannot be ignored. The mind cannot accept to cut our relationship with Iran because it's a super power that ensures the stability in the Middle East, and has interest in Africa and will not stand against us. Our security cooperation continues and we have kept it for our stability. There is alliance between Turkey, Qatar and Iran.

Following the current expulsion of the IS organizations from Syria and Iraq and because there are no suitable terrain to continue their struggle, some of them want to head to Asia and others want to go to West Africa. We must find them sanctuary in South Sudan Areas of Bahr al Ghazal and Western Equatoria in order to continue their struggle. These areas will link them to Boko Haram through CAR and some of them we are going to use them in Libya.

General Backri Hassan Salih

What had happened in the SPLM-N is the result of its internal political contradictions and organizations and the absence of peace vision. Everything was available for Agar and Arman to continue to achieve political settlement with the government from the beginning of the National Dialogue Conference. But obsessions of struggle and attempting to study the reality on opposite sides led them to a blocked road that will not go to anywhere and at the end they accept to split. They were having a chance to sign an agreement and put Hilu into trouble and eventually forced him through the AU mediator to give in. We consulted Agar and Arman for all guarantees if they sign the agreement. They said to us, "Wait", we will sign soon because Hilu mislead them and finally took the command when the situation is ripe, prior to the Nuba Liberation Council meeting that Hilu used against them. Basically, Hilu wants to split Sudan, but he comes at the wrong time. We will make him to fail, dislodge him from Nuba Mountains and return the leadership of the movement to Agar.

This is the plan keeping the unity of Sudan and eliminating the SPLA-N. The government and its institutions will work to weaken the supporters of Hilu through military, political and security means. For example, in Blue Nile we will create disputes between them and divide them based on their tribal affiliations, then eliminate them militarily with the cooperation of Agar forces to dislodge them from the areas they control. The SPLA-N in the Blue Nile is weak. We will benefit from the cooperation of the sons of Angassana to defeat Hilu supporters. But in South Kordofan the sons of Nuba that hate Hilu are many; therefore, we will conduct infiltration operations and recruit all those who hate Hilu. The senior commanders that refused to join Agar will be considered as the first-degree enemies.

Hilu was able to impose his will and control the SPLM-N by occupying the position of leadership with strict control, bold skill and the absence of Agar and Arman. This does not mean that he is victorious. He only snatched the SPLM-N through launching of discrimination and the idea of self-determination to strengthen his base through his tribal wing and the tribes of Aduck. Through Nuba he occupied the leadership of the SPLM-N movement. There is a new approach that Hilu be could relied on to promote the political objective of his movement and in the way that suits the current regional and international situation.

Hilu is dreaming of realizing his plan of self-determination, something that Nubans and all those supporting them will pay high price to achieve this objective. The reality is that Hilu's political speech is based on discrimination that makes no way for Nuba, Aduck and Burun to remain in Blue Nile. There is no place for Hilu in Blue Nile and he could not speak of negotiations. If each area is separated, it will scatter Hilu's ideas so that he cannot create supporters. We must move Sudan Call Forces against him through Sadiq al Mahdi, make people have no confidence in Hilu and move regional and international players against him by convincing them that he rejected peace.

To complete lifting of sanctions we will concentrate on putting pressure on Saudi Arabia to convince US President to lift of sanctions completely. Lifting of sanctions brings a big political victory to the NCP and defeat to rebels and oppositions that dreaming of regime change. If the sanction is completely lifted the rest is easy. According to my judgments, the Americans and Europeans would not neglect their security for the benefit of few people called activities in America.

A question is: where can they get the intelligence information to combat terrorism, if they do not lift the sanctions? We will stop cooperation with them on intelligence, combating of illegal immigration, human trafficking and money laundering if they do not lift the sanctions. We need the suspending of the ICC case and the removal of Sudan from the list of the states supporting of terrorism.

As following the slow motion politics of Gulf crisis, we will continue to supply Qatar with food. For the Gulf crisis, we would not take a particular position but support finding solutions.

Our interest with Qatar in Libya is continuing and supports all Islamists to destroy Hafter and disrupt Egyptian interests in Libya with continuous deployment of our forces along Libya-Egyptian borders. We intend to control the situation inside South Sudan until American sanctions are lifted, will not open humanitarian corridors, will increase the production of oil to prevent Salva Kiir from defeating his opponents and will support Darfur movements in South Sudan and in Egypt. Salva Kiir's goal is not to lift Sudan's sanctions, but they do not know that Sudan possess information that the US with its capabilities cannot obtain it.

Sudan is under threat. We will use all available options to punish Salva Kiir and Hilu in a suitable time. Instructors and those in charge of recruitment are to recruit from the International University of Africa. It's very necessary to find students of South Sudan who are members of the IS to provide assistances to those coming from Middle East in jungles.

Professor Ibrahim Ghandour

The idea of relocating the extremist organizations to South Sudan could link them with many places. The area could link them to the West Africa with Boko Haram and to the East with Somalia. The sanctions could be lifted according to reports handed over to White House on Sudan's efforts to reach American agreement to lift sanctions. But there are no clear answers about the reality of decisions of US Administration on the lifting of sanctions or maintaining them. The final decision remains in the hands of President Donald Trump.

We must move extensively our activities with Saudi Arabia, Emirates and Congress and with some of Sudan's friends in America. The committee must meet for security and intelligence consultation and hold out extensive meetings to establish measures and regulations for the areas we have not executed, for example, problems of the South Sudan and passing of humanitarian aid, peace in the two areas and Darfur, and collecting facts about South Sudan and movements through documenting. But the issue of terrorism is simple. We can stop two planned terrorist attacks before their execution in Europe or against American interest. This will be a good achievement. And prepare ourselves with intelligence to surprise Americans. To make them hungry for information, then we will continue cooperation.

The meeting in Atlantic City of America will be on July 8 a few days from the date President Trump will carry out his decisions. We invited Sudan alliance, called representatives of Sudan government. The problem is how representing the SPLM-N following the split. We must forward a suggestion that SPLM-N should be represented by two delegations: Agar and Hilu groups that could be invited through Carter Center that the US State Department requested to make last efforts to reinstate the negotiations between the Sudanese parts regarding the humanitarian issue, stop escalation of tension and move to the road toward negotiations to peace settlement.

During our last meeting with the representative of the US and Norwegian envoys in Oslo, we looked at the developments of relations between Sudanese, US and Europe to ensure our capabilities to eradicate terrorism in Europe, Africa and Asia and support us financially. We looked at lifting of economic sanctions, removal of Sudan from the list of states supporting terrorism, suspending the ICC indictments and ensuring that Sava Kiir does not get peace in his country through convincing evidences. He has to return to negotiations with all his opponents.

Talk about the relationship between Sudan and South Sudan on the five areas and confirm that the problems of South cannot resolve because of Salva Kiir supports armed movements, proofed with documenting evidence. Talk about the difficulty of achieving peace in the two areas, passing of humanitarian aid because of split of SPLM-N into two groups. Hilu refuses negotiations and Salva Kiir provides him with assistances. Hilu is demanding self-determination of the two areas and wants to attach them to South Sudan in the current situations of South Sudan. Hilu and Salva Kiir want to prolong the war and hinder the existence of Sudan. The international community must know the intension of Hilu.

We believe Agar is closer to peace and the Troika group supports their plan and encourages the AU to support their cause because the Angassana people are the ones who have problems and need solutions. Sudan needs economic sanctions to be completely lifted. Then, it can execute the following five areas, the cooperation of combating terrorism, illegal immigration to Europe, stop support of Lord Resistance Army (LRA). Regarding our agreement, US suggestion concerning humanitarian aid for the victims in the war zones, our readiness to set in the negotiations with the rebel movements for security arrangements and make complete cease fire and then enter into negotiations and make political settlement but the rebels refused. There is increasingly belief in US institutions such as intelligence, State Department to see it necessary to take a political approach to maintain the Sudan government, but still there are some legislative groups that put pressure to continue the use of sanctions. Each group has its reasons and views and its consequences.

Those supporting the reduction of sanctions have achieved visible developments. Regarding changing of our foreign strategy was we cut relations with Iran and enter into new alliances with US allies in Middle East cooperation with US intelligence in charge of combating illegal immigration to Europe. Second, lifting of economic sanctions is a credit to paying Sudan for its increasing cooperation on these areas, improving human rights records and settling the internal disputes through peaceful ways.

The reasons of those who not support us see that Sudan government gained achievements in the foreign policy but have not achieved developments in resolving the internal problems, respecting human rights, stopping the war in Darfur, south Kordofan and Blue Nile. The evaluation of the five areas will not depend only in the position of the international community policies. As a result, the internal politics depends on resolving humanitarian assistances, armed conflicts despite the fact the Sudan government will be held responsible alone. As a result, the Sudan's internal policy is weak compared to what we achieved on addressing regional and international community.

The renewal of war in Darfur, arrest of activities, demolition of Churches and arrest of priests among others are examples. The positive US evaluations would increase the reductions of sanctions, would be encouraging. Even in the situation of carrying out American positive evaluation of lifting economic sanctions will put us in a long road until complete relations with the two countries are fully established. Then we will remain with two problems: Removing of Sudan from the list of states supporting of terrorism in the America foreign affairs and find ways to negotiate to settle the issue of list of terrorism in all parts. The issue of ICC and its complete solution is also important.

Split of SPLM-N means split of works inside is born of two new movements. One is under the leadership of Agar and the other under the leadership of Hilu. The plan that will take us to peace there must be separation of tribes in the movement. This way probably will escalate into serious internal fighting and confrontation similar to the one occurred in Blue Nile.

Split of SPLM-N comes after the failure of an internal political efforts attempted by Jogot Mokuar and Ahmed Umda. There are regional intervention from South Sudan and political parts. The problem that causes disputes in the leadership of the armed conflict that cause huge loses to both sides and weakens the SPLA-N. The NCP gains the destructions of its opponents. We have experience in negotiations of split movements and come out with minor loses from negotiating table.

Agar and Arman will negotiate in the problems of the Blue Nile area. Some nationalists will be used to achieve some political positions, even if it's limited. Hilu and his allies, Blue Nile, will hold on to find solutions to the two areas. They will strongly hold to maintain the SPLA-A and self-determination. This problem will hinder the issue of peace. Hilu's position is far from political reality. We can put him under the regional and international pressure that would lead to his political isolation and make him to remain in Nuba Mountains. Inform the parts that Hilu can have no option but to sign peace or be killed in internal conflicts or through our military forces.

Hilu caused Sudan huge destructions. He began with Bolad rebellion and continues rebels and become persisting headache and threating the security of Sudan. Our position regarding Gulf crisis should be impartial and help to resolve the problem through Kuwait mediation. The SPLM-N failed to adopt a national project instead participate in the split of the South Sudan and supported war in Darfur. Failure of his leadership in South Sudan and his weak cadres we could be recruited, if the economic sanctions are lifted we welcome it, if not lifted we must liberate our land. The Blue Nile becomes weak we conquer it first and dislodge Hilu's supporters. What will be remaining to us is South Kordofan and we will conduct siege against them until they surrender. We will not leave one inch of the remaining land of the Sudan. End the existence of SPLA-A. There is sufficient information.

To guarantees their future, Agar and his group can help us to isolate Hilu. This is very important in the coming period his forces can be infiltrated by Agar's group. There are those that reject Hilu that must be taken care of and we will give them employment and they can work against whoever supporting him. Our Army is capable.

The cease fire gave us an opportunity to train thousands of soldiers and prepare them with modern fighting equipment. It is a good for Sudan not to declare his position so that not to be at the cost of the state Qatar as our strategic ally. We need assistance from Saudi Arabia to lift American sanctions. Egyptians need us to make our declaration. Saudi Arabia and Emirates fear our presence and support of Muslims Brothers in Libya and we will not let Hafter become president in Libya. Whatever support they provide him, he will fail like the failure of Salva Kiir in controlling the government of South Sudan. We will make Libya under fire for Khalifa Hafter.

Hafter is supported by the government from Eastern Libya. We will continually create crisis for him in Libya and to make problems escalate through creating a number of crises to gain additional time. The government of National Concord of Libya succeeded in creating new political balance, but has not succeeded in a number of areas. Ending the role of Hafter in the national army and appoint a new commander is among many other issues. There is a competition between

Europeans, Arabs and Egypt. They want US Administration to give them the right to intervene for the benefit of Hafter.

Egypt and Emirates are playing a bad role by supplying Hafter with arms to prolong the Libyan crisis. We must consolidate Islamists to defeat Hafter. But for South Sudan, we must create problems for it with specialized organizations with multiple objectives. These will support the creation of conflicts.

Teacher Hamid Momtuz

We have ensured our cooperation with AU in combating terrorism and extremism and Sudan is ready to offer its experiences in the areas of combating terrorism and treaties, its root causes, with African countries. Presence of extremists in South Sudan, CAR, Uganda and Congo will succeed because of the lack of financial capabilities of these countries.

There are some new developments inside SPLM-N in which Hilu declared self-determination. To defeat this plan administered by the country of South Sudan, we need to isolate Hilu from political work with tactics and plans to deceive him, and then, neutralize him especially when he wants the partition of Sudan into five countries. There is a need to determine to know him through Agar. All sons of South Kordofan do not like Hilu, even Mubarak Ardul refused to support his leadership. Hilu and his group have no place in Sudan. Therefore, it does not need to give them care. Their dreams will not be realized.

The problem of Qatar-Saudi Arabia with their allies is a complicated crisis. It required us to take a position on where our interest is rather than following emotions. Despite the pressures from Saudi Arabia on us to determine our position, we have only to manipulate them until our sanctions are lifted. Sisi is the one putting pressure to put Sudan into trouble, but we should ignore him. Our forces should continue to maintain our commitment in Yemen and try to avoid any situation reducing our efforts in the lifting of economic sanctions. Our positions would be to maintain the two, Qatar and Saudi Arabia.

General Mohamed Atta al Mola

Make a strategy to lift economic sanctions and this strategy will result in facts that in the end issue executive orders to partially lift the sanctions and a parallel strategy to remove Sudan from the list of states supporting terrorism. Before I talk about this strategy, what is important is that the Americans are not sure that Sudan is supporting terrorism and how it participated in it's funding. Even the accusations of Nairobi and Dar al Salam bombing of American Embassies and USS Colc in Yemen have no evidence. These are just accusations only.

The Americans have no facts to base these claims on which put Sudan in the list of states supporting terrorism. They mentioned Osama bin Laden was in Sudan and Emat Macnia who was in charge of Hezbollah military intelligence and Sudan provided sanctuary to Joseph Kony, the leader of LRA. Terrorism in Sudan was persistent in the way of threatening Americans. It is because of the reasons of presence of terrorists and because passing of terrorists. It is true Sudan is facilitating financial aid to groups of terrorists. But we tell them that Sudan have no knowledge of supporting terrorism. If you have information tell us, we are ready to combat terrorism and assure our desire to cooperate with you.

Sudan began to make laws and procedures to combat terrorism and money laundering. There is evidence that we have created an internal office about a year ago to combat money laundering in Sudan. This office is established to help us come out from black list. These are actions clearly indicating our efforts in combating and financing of terrorists. This certificate proved that Sudan does not support and host terrorist groups and making clear efforts to prevent financial assistance and passing of terrorist funds. These are the efforts that made the international financial control group remove Sudan from its black list. This base resulted into partial lifting of the economic sanctions. The parts agreed on the five tracks. These include, combating LRA, peace in South Sudan, passing humanitarian aid. Ethiopian Sudan made efforts to bring peace in South Sudan if Salva Kiir had not refused to make agreement with Riek Machar and arriving of humanitarian assistances. Sudan made efforts to bring peace in Darfur, Blue Nile and South Kordofan but the failure came as a result of rebel movements rejecting peace.

Sudan efforts in combating terrorism are clear and good. Relations with our neighbors are also good. The need is to concentrate on development and find solutions to economic difficulty. Sudan cut its relations with Iran and Hamas and strengthened its relations with Saudi Arabia and Gulf countries. The relationship between Sudan and Saudi Arabia and Gulf states comes at the cost of Iran. Respect our commitments and offer what is required of us, but the continuation of war in Darfur and the two areas comes as the result of rebels refusing the peace. We can build a good strategy to avoid economic crisis that can put us in a black list.

Removing the name of Sudan from the list of states supporting terrorism will be in agreement with this strategy that remains strong and suitable for further execution into the near future. The rest is the matter of time. And we must show political will for the American Administration. We gained the confidence of the intelligence because their information on Sudan is poor and we understood the way they operate and explained events. Sudan offered them information that no country in the world has provided them. It is important to concentrate to cooperate with them at present moment and in the future. The Gulf crisis between Qatar, Saudi Arabia, Egypt, Bahrain and Emirate is an old issue but is renewed. We have to be impartial because Saudi interest in US is huge and it's a partner of America.

We have to bend to Saudi Arabia because we are facing sanctions and that need to be lifted. The American intelligence is cooperating with and indicated in report for the US Administration to lift sanctions. Saudi Arabia and Emirate intelligences all are on our side. Let's be ready to face the period after the lifting of sanctions because we will be a free country determine our relations and no one can dictate to us what to do.

The disagreement of SPLM-N and its split is a victory for NCP. Take Agar as good and Hilu as bad. All capabilities must be used to serve our objectives inside the SPLM-N in the two areas. Split and separate Blue Nile region from South Kordofan. Start to establish a large security and intelligence base to recruit thousands of informants from Nuba, sons opposing Hilu, build a spying base through security cells inside Nuba Mountains and assign agents to follow the movement of Hilu daily and senior commanders of SPLM-N to see if he starts to appoint his deputy, Secretary General and his assistants in the secretaries. We have to have presence in all SPLA-N units because the split provides an opportunity to move membership from one side to other. If any organization experiences split, its infiltration and dismantling will be easy. Determine the means and watch everything happening. We have experience with Darfur movements. From now on, we make an intelligence file to gather the means to accomplish intelligence collection from sources and make specific spying equipment. Better for NCP to support Agar and Arman because they are closer to us.

General Ibrahim Mohamed al Hassan

Split inside SPLM-N between Hilu on one side and Agar and Arman on the other is a struggle for existence. Hilu sees himself as the spiritual father of Nuba Mountains and felled that things move in the opposite direction. His hopes in the Nuba Mountains since his failure to win the state elections and Nuba split against on him. Senior leaders of Nuba Mountains rejected him. Ismael Jalab, Telephone Koko, Daniel Kodi and Tabita Butrus supported the election of Telephone Koko. They considered him representative of Nuba. Hilu exempted them from the leadership of the movement and started a war in which he cannot achieve a victory. This time he imposed new conditions and that go high by exploiting some hopeless people from Nuba Mountain to execute his agenda that to separate Nuba Mountain to form a country that would be ruled by him.

After that he will start to support rebellion in other regions until divide Sudan into five countries. This will be a dangerous plan. NCP and the Islamic Movement must make a strategy to counter his plan and eventually to make it fail. This plan also has special consideration from South Sudan. Agar and Arman are good minded and soft in their approach to resolve the problem of the two areas to make Sudan united. They make security arrangements and DDR to SPLA-N. We hold on Agar's approach in negotiations. If the Agar groups were not late they would have signed peace and blocked the road to Hilu. He would not be able to turn against them. Things are clear now and groups are set and anyone can determine his position for the unity of Sudan and SAF remaining as a national army.

The SPLA was united and our intelligence information on its movements was limited during operations. Now, followed the split there is a lot of information. The SPLA in Blue Nile is composed of different tribes of Burun and Aduck; the majority of them are Christians. The tribes of Watweed, Surkum, Dawala and Berti are Muslims. The Angassana army is outside the area and they support Agar. In this situation, split is easy. I agree to dismantle SPLA-A in Blue Nile first and work on to dismantle those of Hilu.

Divide Nuba and dismantle them and create problems that should lead them to fighting internal wars in the areas they control. Control each group through SAF and the problem should be created between Hilu and Nuba Liberation Council and between Hilu and the Association of Nuba Sons. Create problems between SPLM-N external offices with commanders in the operational areas. Make Hilu relieve Jogot Mockuar and Ezat Koko of duty and create problem division between SPLA-N Division Commanders and Brigades on tribal bases. Create rebellion of Moro, Atoro, Hiban and the tribes in the western region, the tribes of Agant who are Muslims and tribes of Chad. Make plans in Nuba Mountains to make Nuba sons to broadly feel bad about the situations in operational areas and power and tribal balance.

Take into consideration the Churches of Christian tribes and spread the problems from the disputes usually in the Churches through skilled trained agents because the Churches gather all the Christians despite that they are agreed or disagree. The benefits of disputes in SPLM-N and SPLA-N make recruiting agents very easy. There are those that belong to Agar group and Arman and they are large group composed of Nuba, Blue Nile, Northerners and Darfuris. They see Hilu and SPLA stopped their interest and future political objectives. And they look for their self-interest. We can gain their support to eliminate our enemy. Hilu and senior leaders of SPLA in the two areas and the military commanders will take over after finished with our enemy.

After making the plan and its secret explanations, we should leave how to execute it to intelligence since information is required from them. Collect all telephones numbers of the military commanders and political leaders of the two areas. Collect telephones numbers of soldiers and non-commissioned officers, civilian administrators and members of the Nuba Liberation Council. Collect emails of all leaders and ways of communications and maintenance garages and command headquarters and names and telephones of bodyguards. Understand types of command and their location, routes, passages, ways of movements, how leaders travel and activities. All we need to know logistics support, rations, organizations, countries that provide support, intelligence organizations, regional and international bodies that support Hilu and his group. We will reveal the type of assistants, intelligence and political support and secret alliances that exist.

We will find out the role of Churches and assistance coming from South Sudan and types of assistance possibly coming from Uganda, America, Israel, UK, Norway and European countries. We will find out if there is assistance that comes from groups of activists or from the movement and funds from the Bank of Nuba Mountain and Nuba sons on the outside. We will find out if there are war efforts to collect rations to send to the groups of Joseph Taka and Jundi Sulman and the situation of negotiations. We will find out about countries, intelligence organizations, personalities that stand behind Hilu to divide Nuba into five countries. We will find out about support to establish Nuba country regionally and internationally. We will look for the types of training and types of courses for commanders of SPLA. We will know the relations between Darfur movements with Hilu and the channels of supporters of Hilu inside Sudan areas. We are required to use Agar group to realize these objectives. We need to know Agar and Arman group well in a very short period of time to make plans and strategies against SPLA-N Hilu faction.

Provide protection and sanctuary to Muslim Brothers, Islamic organizations and all cadres will continue to provide them with training youth in the **International African University**. Provide with knowledge and continue to provide them with training the youth to become active and their countries to create a radical Islamic branch in South Sudan to use in the time they would need it. The land in South Sudan encourages creating extremist groups if they have their own sanctuary.

Engineer Ibrahim Mahmmoud

Following the collapse of the three leaders of SPLM-N for the reasons of diverse opinions regarding negotiations with the government, the SPLA-N needs to make regime change by fighting a war until their objectives are achieved. Hilu and all Nuba Mountain rebels have the goal to make a regime change and disrupt the future of Sudan. After they failed in political negotiations, Hilu returned to the self-determination. This demand is difficult for him to achieve. Most of Nuba people do not support him. Hilu and his army have no right to impose their will on others. In South Kordofan, the Nuba people do not make the majority of the population. But they are part of the inhabitants. We teach them a lesson.

The NCP will start large campaign to all tribes of South Kordofan and tell them that rebels want to take your land with the use of force. They want to chase you away from South Kordofan. We can force all the tribes in South Kordofan to withdraw their sons fighting with Nuba rebels immediately by political work that is well organized.

We will make a media campaign with the objective to worsen the situation inside SPLA-N and dismantle SPLA-A creating rebel factions from Nuba sons to work against Hilu in order to stop this revolution and the movement. We will disrupt their negotiations by bringing a great many people from Agar group and demand negotiations. If we are able to dismantle them before negotiations is good. What is important is to concentrate crisis in the SPLA in the two areas -very important. This will allow the government and the NCP to find the alternative because members of SPLM and SPLA will unite if Hilu group is dismantled. Basically, Nuba and Blue Nile people do not hate Agar and Arman. This problem only created by Hilu. Even Jalab, Telephone Koko and Kodi are liked in the Nuba Mountains but Hilu annihilated them.

Hilu told Agar to expel Jalab from the movement because they later discovered that Agar has no problem with them. Our relations are good with Malik Agar and Arman; there is a common ground between the NCP and us. The SPLA we extend interest between us. Because of the reasons of this relationship there was a crisis that emerged inside SPLA, which brought a new threat and the presence of SPLA in Nuba Mountains and Blue Nile. The force of infiltration we achieved in negotiation convinced Agar and Arman to seek political settlement through negotiations with the mediation of Germany, France and Ethiopia. Since that time, we discovered that the idea of new Sudan is a big lie. The National Dialogue Conference should be the only basis of governance in Sudan and parliament in the government. It was possible for Agar and Arman to sign an agreement through AU and UN in the presence of envoys of the two countries to put Hilu into trouble. Hilu cannot reject the agreement and keep his place.

The changing of the SPLM-N leadership. This comes at the time of lifting of sanctions and removing Sudan's name from the states supporting terrorism and suspension of ICC indictment. These strategies would have finished the important part of the five corridors for peace. There must be lifting of sanctions because of our efforts and experiences in dismantling armed movements through a program, and we must plan to support the objectives until reconstruction of Sudan. We will not negotiate with Hilu for self-determination to weaken him with scenarios disrupting his group. Most of his leaders in command are ignorant. They do not understand things other than discriminations. This war is to defeat them. We need to determine where their weakness is and do everything possible to exploit and bring back Agar and Arman in political settlements.

As we need to destroy our enemy, Salva Kiir wants to make regime change in Khartoum. We will train youth from South Sudan and from West Africa transferring a group of students supporting Boko Haram from Nigeria because the Sana tribe resembles people who live around Wau and Western Equatoria and let Salva Kiir be faced with a secret movement.

Professor Ibrahim Omer

Qatar has influence in making decisions in the Arab world and Africa. This is one of the dangerous periods coming during the Arab spring supported demonstrations and disturbances, revolutions and military interventions and government in Sudan, Libya, Egypt, Somali, and Tunis. Supporting Muslim Brothers, they become famous with different structures. The diplomacy of Qatar played a big role in maintaining the Islamist government in Sudan. If Qatar and Iran had not assisted, the Sudan government would have failed and they would have arrested us, put us in prisons and killed us. Islamic organizations and Muslim Brothers provided us with financial and moral support and information about organizations opposing Islamic government in Sudan.

The political Islam in Sudan gained wide variety of experiences in all areas of education, and experiences of our Muslim Brothers and global Islamic organization. They want to finish the role of Qatar to benefit the Kingdom of Saudi Arabia and Emirate through American directives. This normally happens in the regions where policies are dictated by other countries. The ruling family in Qatar holds its position and has a united facing of this crisis.

The Gulf countries committed mistake in Syria, so this not in Qatar alone. If the Islamic movements succeeded in Syria, they would have extended their influence to Gulf countries and created crisis. The Gulf countries entered Syria and created problems in Yemen, which is near Libya and Egypt, to stop Islamists.

Qatar supported Islamists when every they are threatened them in every corner of the earth. Sudan is part of the Islamic movement organization. Our role will be limited to impartiality by trying to solve the problem through our relations with Saudi Arabia and continue participating with our force in Yemen. This is the right position in the present movement. Because Sudan is facing the problem of sanctions and it wants them to be completely lifted. Saudi Arabia and Emirates have good alliances with US and Israel. Sudan wanted them to urge Americans to lift the sanctions completely at this time. Support of Islamist is our obligation especially our role in Libya to prevent Hafter coming to rule.

Very important to infiltrate IS into South Sudan in certain areas of Western Bahr al Ghazal and Western Equatoria after finding suitable people to provide them local guidance and security.

The SPLM-N after Hilu took control of it must be weakened, dismantled, divided into several groups in order to facilitate negotiations. Hilu should not impose his conditions and instability and continue war but the situation has changed.

Recommendations

1. Ensure the continuation of participation of our forces in Yemen
2. Present our role in the alliance of combating terrorism
3. Make a plan to relieve Hafter of control of Libya
4. Make a strategy on how to employ the information on terrorism to the benefit of our higher interests
5. Make a strategy with multiple faces to dismantle and destroy SPLM-N
6. Facilitate transferring of money and leaders of IS to West Africa
7. Facilitate Islamist of IS and al Qaeda to infiltrate Libya and Egypt
8. Make a complete study on how to bring Islamic movements to South Sudan
9. Separate Blue Nile from South Kordofan through creating problems between the two
10. Create a security committee to establish a strategy to Isolate Hilu politically
11. Continue to cooperate with Agar group
12. Be impartial in addressing Gulf crisis
13. Provide secure sanctuaries for the Islamist leaving Qatar
14. Put pressure on Saudi Arabia to coordinate with US President to completely lift the sanctions from the Sudan
15. Ensure our cooperation with intelligence on combating terrorism
16. Continue our cooperation with Europe to combat illegal immigration, money laundering, removing Sudan from the list of countries supporting of terrorism and suspend the issue of ICC through the UNSC.

Appendix D
A US attempt to get the Truth,
A Sudan attempt to find the resistance,

Arrests follow

Following Special Envoy Donald Booth's visit to the town of Nertiti, a Sudan Activist now living in the US, Abdalhaleim Hassan wrote this plea on Facebook.

Darfur Misery and Obama's Silence

By Abdalhaleim Hassan, activist originally from Darfur, Sudan
August 2, 2016

More than 16 leaders have been arrested after their meeting with Donald Booth, the U.S Special Envoy to both Sudan and South Sudan The Government accused them of being members of a resistance movement.

During the current visit of Donald E. Booth, the U.S. Special Envoy for the Sudan and South Sudan. Donald had several meetings with the IDPs leaders in many camps in Darfur, Zalingei, Elfasir, and Kass. In Nertiti, Booth had met them in the headquarters of the African Union - United Nations Mission in Darfur [UNAMID]. Victims have reported their tragedies caused by the current ongoing genocide in Darfur and the absence of security. Furthermore, they have told Donald their stories and their worries of daily killing, rape women and violence against the human rights across Darfur. They complained about the rights of their land, the replacement issue by the newcomers. After the meetings on July 28, 2016 many of the attendees were arrested on July 31 and it's continue in Kass, Zalingei and Nertiti, Darfur. Here are some that were arrested:
- Alrasheed Eissa an employee of the UNAMID in Nertiti and the community leader in the area also known as (Mayor) in the United States. The story told by witness that Eissa and two others were asked by the government agency not to give any details about the situation, (misinterpret) during their job as an interpreters at the UNAMID the head quarter in Nertiti. But the Special Envoy had their own interpreters. Later, Mr. Eissa arrested on August 1st
- Adam Siding, the head of Northern Nertiti IDPs Comps Committee
- Abdelkarim Adam, the head of the Southern Nertiti IDPs Comps committee- 66 years old
- Mohamed Suliman, IDP
- Adam Hamid, IDP
- Naser Eldin Yousif - IDP
- Adam Mohamed, IDP
- Adam Musa, IDP 50 years old
- Eltigani Abdelgabar Yousif, the local clinics assistant 65 years old

I am asking the U.S. Special Envoy for immediate action to free the detainees and insure their safety. Furthermore, I am very sure Ambassador Booth is an eyewitness of the situation in Darfur and the reactions of the Sudanese Government by arresting all victims and leaders who were met with Booth. I am asking the recognition that we are asking for the US to help stop the genocide in Sudan instead of letting the Sudanese Government continue committing their crimes. The people of Sudan are asking for real help to stop the genocide.

Situation after August 29, 2017

These 9 were arrested after meeting with Special Envoy Booth, but have since been released. They continue to be at risk. Some have had their property confiscated and some have been banned from Nertiti by the government. We hope that the government of Sudan can be pressured to leave them alone.

1- Abdelkarim Adam Abdelkarim
2- Adam sideg Abdalla Terab
3- Eltigani Yousif Abdelgabar
4- Ishag Adam Abdelshafi
5- Alrasheed Mohamed Eissa
6- Yahya Mohamed Yousif
7- Adam Ishag Abdelkarim
8- Osman Abdelgadir Abdel Sadig
9- Adam Mohamed Musa

These 7 were arrested after meeting with Special Envoy Booth and are still in detention. We hope that the government of Sudan can be pressured to release them and leave them alone.

10- Ali Abdelaziz Ali - known as Abu-halla
11- Ahmed suliman - know as Santana
12- Mohamed Eltigani Saif-eldeen
13- Adam Hamid Adam - a Nertiti camp leader
14- Adam Mohamed Ali - a Nertiti camp leader
15- Nasr-Eldin Yousif Abdalla
16- Ahmed Abdalla Omar

In addition to the 16 who were arrested, above, these additional 7 IDP leaders have been arrested in the Kass IDP Camps. Although these leaders did not meet with Special Envoy Booth in Nertiti, they coordinated with the IDPs who did meet with Booth. We hope that the government of Sudan can be pressured to release them and leave them alone.
17- Adam Salih, head of the Shawa IDP camp
18- Khalil Adam Ibrahim
19- Omar Abdelkarim
20- Abdelgabar Ahmed Abdelmawla, Alhomiera primary school manager
21- Abdalla Mondi

22- Alhadi Ishag Mohamed, instructor
23- Osman Ibrahim Abdel-Shakor

Lastly, IDP leaders in Zalingei and Sortoni are being pursued by the government and are at risk of arrest. We are not mentioning their names now, but hope that the government of Sudan can be pressured to leave them alone.

References

Chapters

1 - Could Sudan be the cornerstone of the Caliphate in Africa?

"Sudan", November 11, 2016, Radio, Tamazui.

Eric Reeves, "Sudan in the Wake of a Trump Victory", November 15, 2016, *Sudan Tribune.*

Mahmoud A. Suleiman, "Bashir's call for mutual cooperation with U.S. Trump", November 13, 2016, Sudan *Tribune.*

The New Arab, "Sudan Opposition calls for 3-day strike over fuel prices", *November 27, 2016*

Jerry Gordon, "Only Regime Change Can Stop Sudan's Genocide: interview with Gen. Abakar M. Abdallah ", *New English Review,* November 2016.

Zaghawa People, Wikipedia.

Ansar Dine, Mali, Tracking Terrorism & Analysis Consortium.

SELEKA rebels, Central Africa Republic, *Britannica.*

Sudan People's Liberation Movement, South Sudan, Wikipedia.

Ali Tamim-Fatak, *Africa Sustainable Conservation.*

National Liberation Movement for Liberation of Azawad. Wikipedia

"Sudan, Saudi Arabia expect to earn $ 20 billion from Atlantis II project", May 2, 2016, *Sudan Tribune.*

Eleonora Ardemagni, The Yemeni Factor in the Saudi Arabia Sudan Realignment", April 2016, *The Arab Gulf States Institute.*

ibid, "Only Regime Change Can Stop Sudan's Genocide", **New English Review**, November 2016.

2 - Peacemaking Calumny.

Donald Booth, "Peace in Sudan must not be held hostage to Abdul Wahid," November 22, 2016, Sudan *Tribune.*

3 - President Obama's Folly: Executive Order 13761 Lifting Sudan Sanctions.

President Barack Obama, "Executive Order 13761— Recognizing Positive Actions by the Government of Sudan and Providing for the Revocation of Certain Sudan-Related Sanctions", American Presidency Project, January 13, 2017.

Eric Reeves, "The Final Betrayal of Sudan: Obama administration's lifting of economic sanctions; UN Ambassador Samantha Power justifying the move, claiming a "sea change" of improvement in humanitarian access, " January 14, 2017, *HuffPost*.

Mike Brand, "Obama's upsetting decision to lift sanctions on Sudan, January 13, 2017", *The Hill*.

Felicia Schwartz and Martina Stevis, "U.S., Altering Course, Moves to Lighten Sanctions Against Sudan", January 13, 2017, Wall Street Journal.

US Rep. James Mc Govern, "McGovern Statement on New Obama Sanctions Policy for Sudan", January 13, 2017.

"120 US Congress Members Call on President Obama to Keep Sudan Humanitarian Crisis a high priority," May 5, 2016, Radio Dabanga.

Joseph Trevithick, "A Guide to the Pentagon's Shadowy Network of Bases in Africa", March 1, 2017, *The War Zone*.

"U.S. Congressman accuses Sudan of obstructing humanitarian access, "March 4, 2017, *Sudan Tribune*.

Ian Allen, "Top aide to Trump's security adviser denied security clearance by CIA", Intelnews.org, February 13, 2017.

4 - President Bashir perpetrates Jihad.

Jerry Gordon, "Jihad in Darfur: 18 Killed — 76 Wounded in Sudan 'Peace Forces' New Year Attacks by Lt. Gen. Abakar M. Abdallah", January 8, 2017, Fitnaphobia.

5 - Revealed: Bashir's Secret Jihad Plan for Sudan.

Sir Winston S. Churchill, *The River War: An Account of the Reconquest of the Sudan*, 1899.

Lt. Gen. (ret.) Abakar M. Abdullah, Jerry Gordon, Deborah Martin, "The Secret Radical Islamic Document found in Darfur, Sudan", Dr. Rich Swier blog, February 15, 2017.

6 - Political Islam in Sudan supported by Qatar, the UAE and Saudi Arabia.

"Leading Sudanese Jihadist Killed in Libya", July 7, 2016, *Sudan Tribune*.

Islamic Da'wa Organization (Sudan) The Global Daily Muslim Brotherhood Watch.

Union of Good, The CounterJihad Report

International University of Africa, Wikipedia.

Her Highness Sheikha Mozah Bint Nasser, Wikipedia

Hamad bin Khalifa Al Than, **Wikipedia.**

"Sheikha Moza visits pyramids in Sudan restored with Qatar help," **March 13, 2017, The** *Peninsula***, Qatar.**

"Why is the Political Islam in Sudan supported by Gulf Emirates and Saudi Arabia? " **Lt. Gen. Abakar M. Abdallah, March 28, 2017,** *New English Review/Iconoclast.*

7 - Billions for Bashir at Arab League Summit.

"Sudan's Bashir discuss "major investments" with UAE companies", **March 7, 2017,** *Sudan Tribune.*

"Sudan's Bashir, Kuwait's Sabah discusses bilateral relations", **April 12, 2017,** *Sudan Tribune.*

"Gulf countries, Sudan to sign partnership agreement: Bashir", **April 12, 2017, Sudan Tribune.**

US. Rep. James McGovern, "Congressman McGovern Meets with Sudanese Leaders to Discuss Humanitarian Crisis and U.S. Sanctions', **February 28, 2017.**

Jerry Gordon, Lt. Gen. (ret.) Abakar M. Abdallah, Deborah Martin "Billion Dollar Saudi and Emeriti Economic Projects for Sudan President Bashir Revealed at Arab League Summit," **April 10, 2017,** *New English Review/Iconoclast*

8 - The price for lifting US Sudan Sanctions: Genocide.

"36 killed in tribal clashes in North Kordofan", **April 5, 2017, Sudan** *Tribune.*

"Darfur of today is different from 2003: UNAMID head", **April 5, 2017,** *Sudan Tribune.*

"ICC demands investigation of UNAMID in Darfur", **June 18, 2014,** *Radio Dabanga.*

Ahmed Younis, "Former spokesperson renews criticism of UN mission in Darfur," **April 20, 2014,**

Lt. Gen. (ret.) Abakar M. Abdallah, "The price for lifting US Sudan Sanctions: Genocide," **April 9, 2017,** *New English Review/Iconoclast.*

9 - Sudan resistance commanders present the case to Congress on Retaining Sudan Sanction.

US House of Representatives, Subcommittee on Africa, Global Health, Global Human Rights and International Institutions, **Hearing April 26, 2017, The Questionable Case for Easing Sudan Sanctions**

Jerry Gordon and Deborah Martin, "The Questionable Case for Lifting Sudan Sanctions: Testimonies of Sudan Resistance Leaders-Part 1 General Abakar M. Abdallah of Sudan United Movement", **April 29, 2017,** *New English Review/Iconoclast.*

Jerry Gordon and Deborah Martin, "The Questionable Case for Lifting Sudan Sanctions: Testimonies of Sudan Resistance Leaders – Part II Testimony of Gen. General Abdalaziz Adam Alhilu, SPLA/N General commander/Chief of staff of SPLA/N and Deputy Chairman of the SPLM", **April 29, 2017,** *New English Review/Iconoclast.*

Jerry Gordon and Deborah Martin, "The Questionable Case for Lifting Sudan Sanctions: Testimonies of Sudan Resistance Leaders-Part 3 Mr. Sodi Ibrahim, Executive Director of the Sudan Relief and Rehabilitation Agency (SRRA-N) and Yunan Musa Kunda, SSRA-N External Relationship Coordinator", **April 29, 2017,** *New English Review/Iconoclast.*

10- Chad and Libya Cut ties to Qatar and Sudan over support to overthrow Regimes.

Lt. Gen. (ret.) Abakar M. Abdallah, Jerry Gordon, Deborah Martin, "Chad Joins African nations cutting ties to Qatar for support of Terrorism", **June 9, 2017,** *New English Review/Iconoclast.*

"LNA's Mismark Accuses Sudan, Qatar, and Iran of backing terrorism in Libya", **June 22, 2017,** *Libya Herald.*

Jonathan Schanzer, "Qatar's Support of The Worst of the Worst In Libya Must End", **August 6, 2017,** *Newsweek.*

11- Sudan Hires Washington Lobbyist Firm, Human Rights Advocates and Congress Dispute Lifting Sanctions.

Lt. Gen. (ret.) Abakar M. Abdallah, "Was there a failed coup attempt in Khartoum?" **June 28, 2017,** *New English Review/Iconoclast.*

"Report: Sudanese official offered to carry out coup in Qatar", **June 29, 2017,** *Middle East Monitor.*

Robbie Gramer, "Report Sudan Hires U.S. Lobbyist to Roll Back Sanctions, July 7, 2017, Foreign Policy.**

 Greta Van Susteren, MSNBC *For the Record* "Will Trump Let a Brutal Dictator Off the Hook", **June 16, 2017.**

Nuba Reports.

Ryan Boyette**, LinkedIn

Frank Wolf, Wikipedia

Erik Reeves, "Letter to Congress from Former Special Envoys for Sudan, Throwing Their Weight Behind Lifting of Sanctions on Sudan: A Critique," June 30, 2017, SUDAN, Research and Advocacy.

Republic of Sudan, "Minutes of National Political Crisis Committee", June 18, 2017, Khartoum, Arabic original.

Malik Agar, Wikipedia

Ibid, "Why Is Political Islam in Sudan supported by Gulf Emirates and Saudi Arabia?"

Jerry Gordon, "Sudan, Qatar and Iran accused of backing terrorism in Libya", June 23, 2017, *Fitnaphobia.*

John Boehner, *The Hill.*

Squire Paton Boggs, Foreign Agent Registration Act (FARA) filing, US Department of Justice.

Erik Pedersen, "George Clooney Co-Authors Op-Ed On Sudan's Rich Deal With U.S. Lobbying Firm", June 6, 2017, *Deadline Hollywood.*

"Sudan denies hiring U.S. firms to lobby for lifting of sanctions", July 17, 2017, Sudan *Tribune.*

Megan R. Wilson, "Sudan sanctions spur intense lobbying", July 19, 2017, *The Hill.*

"U.S. Treasury allows full resumption of financial transactions with Sudan: minister", July 17, 2017, *Sudan Tribune.*

Matina Stavis, "Sudan gets down to Business in the face of Sanctions and Strife, July 18, 2017", *Wall Street Journal.*

12 - President Trump Signs Order to Defer Lifting Sanctions while Rampage Continues in Darfur.

"Presidential Executive Order on Allowing Additional Time for Recognizing Positive Actions by the Government of Sudan and Amending Executive Order 13761", July 11, 2017 , The White House, President Donald J. Trump.

USCRIF:" SUDAN: USCIRF Urges Secretary of State to Maintain Sanctions ", June 22, 2017.

US Department of State, State Sponsors of Terrorism.

Natalie Johnson, "Humanitarian Advocates Praise Trump's Decision to Postpone Sanctions Relief for Sudan", July 15, 2017, *Washington Free Beacon.*

Michael McHugh, "Surgeon in Sudan civil war wins humanitarian award", May 29, 2017, *The Irish Times.*

Rapid Support Force/Janjaweed (Sudan), Wikipedia.

President Idriss Debye of Chad, Wikipedia.

Libyan National Army, Wikipedia.

"Profile: Libya's military strongman Khalifa Haftar", September 15, 216, *BBC News*.

"Sudan: Hundreds of Darfuri student protesters stopped at the capital's gates", July 19, 2017, *Amnesty International*.

13 - Could a $7.3 Billion Federal Appellate decision against Sudan for 1998 African Embassies upset Sanctions Relief?

"Rescuers search for life in rubble of Nairobi bomb attack", August 8, 1998, *CNN.com.*

Khobar Towers bombing, Saudi Arabia, 1996, Wikipedia.

Megan R. Wilson, "Court upholds multi-billion dollar judgment against Sudan over embassy bombings", July 28, 2017, July 28, 2017.

14 – Sudan President Bashir's 'disarmament' plan in Darfur is cover for Genocide

Lt. Gen (ret.) Abakar M. Abdallah, Jerry Gordon and Deborah Martin, "Sudan President Bashir's 'disarmament' plan in Darfur is cover for Genocide", August 13, 2017, *New English Review/Iconoclast.*

15 -Don't believe your lying eyes: Bashir's deception strategy

Princeton Lyman, Senior Adviser to the President, United State Institute of Peace.Eric Reeves, "New and authoritative translation into English of minutes for August 31 meeting of the most senior military and security officials in the Khartoum regime", October 22, 2014, *SUDAN Research and Advocacy.*

Religion in Sudan, Wikipedia.

Lawrence Joffe, "Hassan al-Turabi Obituary", March 11, 2016, *The Guardian.*

"Rebel group says Sudan inviting Arab Mujahideen to Darfur", August 25, 2006, *Sudan Tribune.*

Eric Reeves, "Comments of particular importance from the leaked minutes of senior level meeting of Khartoum officials, October 11, 2015", SUDAN Research and Advocacy.

"Al Bashir extends ceasefire in Darfur, Two Areas till end 2016", October 11, 2016, *Radio Dabanga.*

"Clarifying the meaning of Dar al-Kufr & Dar al-Islam", March 28, 2008, *TheKhilafah*

16- Can we stop the Sudan Genocide?

About The Authors

Lt. Gen. Abdallah is Chairman of the Sudan Unity Movement. He is a native of North Darfur who joined the Sudan People's Liberation Army (SPLA) in 1984 and became active in the Nuba Mountains and Darfurians resistance movements. In 1989 he joined the Patriotic Salvation Movement in neighboring Chad based in Darfur. He served as an officer in the Chadian army for 23 years. He held senior intelligence and counterterrorism posts including as Coordinator of the Multi-National Joint Task Force of Nigeria, Chad and Niger. He was Coordinator of Pan-Sahel Initiative (PSI) Anti-Terrorism Unit of Chad and Commander of PSI Anti-Terrorism Battalion of Chad 2004. He is a December 2002 graduate of the Intelligence Officers' Advanced and Combating Terrorism Courses, US Army Intelligence Center and Schools, Fort Huachuca, Arizona. He was a Counter Terrorism Fellow and a Graduate of the College of International Security Affairs, National Defense University, Washington, DC, 2005. He was an International Fellow and Graduate of the US Army War College, Class of 2008. He was Graduate of Nigeria Armed Forces Command and Staff College Course 22, of the year 2000.

Jerome B Gordon is a Senior Vice President of the *New English Review* and author of *The West Speaks,* NER Press 2012. Mr. Gordon is a former US Army intelligence officer who served during the Viet Nam era. He was the co-host and co-producer of weekly The Lisa Benson Show for National Security that aired out of KKNT960 in Phoenix Arizona from 2013 to 2016. He is co-host and co-producer of the Middle East Round Table periodic series on 1330amWEBY, Northwest Florida Talk Radio, Pensacola

Deborah Martin is a 36-year veteran linguistics specialist and consultant on Sudan culture and affairs. She is a long-term American Sudan human rights advocate having lived in both North and South Sudan conducting development projects as a professional engineer and linguist in a team with her late husband. She has worked on research linguistics of Jieeng, Nuer, Bari, Jumjum, Masalit, Nubian, Luwo, Reel, Madi and Moro. She has also successfully designed, implemented and led culturally appropriate large and small conferences, seminars and workshops for Sudanese and South Sudanese participants.

www.ingramcontent.com/pod-product-compliance
Lightning Source LLC
Chambersburg PA
CBHW072135270326
41931CB00010B/1764